DEVELOPMENT OF ACCOUNTING THOUGHT

DEVELOPMENT OF ACCOUNTING THOUGHT

HARVEY T. DEINZER *theodore*, *1908–*

University of Florida

Holt, Rinehart and Winston, Inc.
New York · Chicago · San Francisco · Toronto · London

To pioneer teachers of theory in
accounting—such leaders as W. A. Paton,
A. C. Littleton, E. L. Kohler,
George Husband, and DR Scott—this book
is appreciatively dedicated.

PREFACE

The purpose of the course of study for which this book is an aid is to stimulate questioning. Without questions there are no answers. And without the right kinds of questions the search for "knowns" will be devious, if not wholly unproductive. Events since 1940 have not demonstrated the correctness of the contention that in the 1930s "the time had come for those interested in theories and principles to cease raising questions and to begin furnishing answers." [1] This syllabus has been written for students whose intellectual needs have not been satisfied by doctrinaire positions which they may have experienced in earlier training in accounting.

The most important use of this syllabus is to help raise certain types of questions which, it is hoped, will provide the accounting student with a taking-off point for intelligent search into problems that involve choices among goals and among resources. Attention is centered on criteria for the selection of rules for the valuation of assets and the calculation of income of those corporate enterprises for whom public reporting is a recognized responsibility. The rules will here generally be designated accounting-treatment rules.

While the entire book may be viewed as an instrument for stimulating inquiry into accounting-treatment rules, there are at the end of each chapter distinctive sets of questions and critical comments. These questions and comments are intended to bring the assigned readings into connection with the main analytic points that are traced within the chapters.

It will become apparent that the writer has relied upon John Dewey's exposition of the method of science as a standard for approaching questions of choice among accounting-treatment rules. His interest in the functional interpretation of logic began in 1939 when he bought and started the reading of John Dewey's *Logic, The Theory of Inquiry*. Since that time many events have occurred which may be characterized as the application of the method of the

---

[1] From the Foreword, by Howard C. Greer, to *An Introduction to Corporate Accounting Standards* by W. A. Paton and A. C. Littleton.

v

natural sciences to the field of human behavior. Accounting literature is referring more often to the scientific method. It is this thread, that the general method used in the physical sciences controls the identification of knowledge in the areas of human behavior, which runs through the several chapters and provides one point of analysis for the indicated readings.

The present syllabus exhibits many crudities of expression and inadequacies in the representation of analytic points of view. The justification for its publication in advance of artistic refinement is in the importance of approaches for accounting research. Many accounting textbooks are including chapters on "accounting theory," and official positions are being taken following certain research activities which will be identified in this book. Are these positions warranted? Have the conclusions been reached in correspondence with the conditions for successful inquiry? If not, the time to analyze the approaches used and the procedures followed is before the conclusions have become reinforced in the institutional framework of accounting. It is hoped that the searching quality of the questions impersonally asked in this book will promote subsequent constructive operations.

Grateful acknowledgment is extended to Dr. George R. Bartlett, Chairman of the Department of Philosophy at the University of Florida, for his encouragement following the reading of an earlier draft and for his careful reading of Chapter 4 of the final draft. The writer expresses his thanks also to Dr. Delmas D. Ray, Professor of Accounting at the University of Florida, for the latter's experimental use of the book in a graduate course in accounting theory shared with the author. The writer, of course, bears the responsibility for the content, and more specifically, for the interpretations of premises and philosophical viewpoints suggested as underlying various positions and proposals appearing in the accounting literature on bases for asset valuation and income computation.

Gainesville, Florida
February 1965   HARVEY T. DEINZER

CONTENTS

Preface   v

Chapter 1
Survey of Accounting Thought and Practice Prior to 1900   1

Chapter 2
An Historical Approach to Accounting Illustrated with
Events since 1900   9

Chapter 3
A Problem Situation for Professional Accountants and
Structures for Organized Accounting Research   17

Chapter 4
Conditions for Knowledge and the Activity of Knowing:
A Reference Standard for Accounting   27

Chapter 5
Conditions for Accounting Theory According to Contem-
porary Accounting Writings   56

Chapter 6
A Particular Framework of Accounting Standards: Re-
flection of the Cost-Allocation Doctrine   73

Chapter 7
Elaboration of the Cost-Allocation Doctrine: Contempo-
rary Accounting "Theory"   85

Chapter 8
The Institute's "New Approach": The Postulates Foundation, and Accounting Research Study No. 1   105

Chapter 9

The Relation of "Broad Principles" to the "Postulates,"
and Accounting Research Study No. 3   122

Chapter 10

Summary of Preceding Chapters and a Projection of the
Institute's Basic Research   141

Chapter 11

Other Lines of Accounting Thought   152

Bibliography   166
Index   175

CHAPTER

1

Survey
of Accounting Thought and Practice
Prior to 1900

"Begin at the beginning" is a time-honored precept. If only one could always know where the beginning is and not wonder about the utility of starting at any point back of the present. If a story is accepted for its own sake, that is, for its literary and artistic value, no date is too far back for a beginning. If past events and practices are viewed for their relevance to current problems, is any nearer point of beginning obvious?

Our survey of the early history of accounting will select principally from two major books in the field: Littleton, *Accounting Evolution to 1900,* and Littleton and Yamey, *Studies in the History of Accounting.*

This first chapter of the syllabus should not be regarded as a miniscule course in accounting history. Some writers have advocated the inclusion of a separate course in accounting history in the accounting curriculum. For example, Homburger ("Study of History —Gateway to Perspective," *The Accounting Review,* July 1958, pp. 501-503) evaluates the study of accounting history by students inclined toward vocational study, and suggests a format for an Accounting History course. It might be argued that, if a full-term course on this subject is valuable, exploration of this type of material for a shorter time duration would yield proportionate benefit. Of course the characteristics of a whole may not be shared by parts of the whole. Yet some brief survey of accounting history might be justified independently. The reader may be interested in pursuing the subject of accounting history as such "on his own."

Approaches to the Study of Accounting History

One obvious approach to the study of history is the division of events into time sequences. Thus the significant periods might be identified as before Paciolo, during Paciolo's time, and developments in England and Scotland coincident with the weakening of the manorial system, the resurgence of art and trade, and movement from household to factory production. But every historical narrative selects from among the myriad of events those conditions and happenings which are relevant to the historian's point of view and to his end in view. The events selected by the historian and the emphases given them are determined by the historian's conception of their relation to intellectual problems set by him.

A typical contrasting emphasis between "the man" and "the institutions" is exemplified in contemporary writings on the history of accounting—you have probably already identified "the man" as Paciolo. Langer, for example ("Paciolo—Patriarch of Accounting," *The Accounting Review*, July 1958, pp. 482-484), extends a reverence for things ancient to the personality of the first expositor of bookkeeping practice. On the other hand, deRoover ("New Perspectives on the History of Accounting," *The Accounting Review*, July 1955, pp. 405-420) subordinates personalities to institutions; de-emphasizes the importance of Paciolo in the history of double-entry bookkeeping; and interprets historical data to yield the conclusion that double-entry bookkeeping developed somewhat spontaneously in various Italian cities as the "combustion point" of business needs was reached.

Guided by a conception of the kinds of events that will be relevant, the historian may attempt to trace the origin and development of a particular idea or practice. This approach is illustrated in an interesting article by deRoover ("The Lingering Influence of Medieval Practices," *The Accounting Review*, April 1943, pp. 148-151) in which the practice dealt with is the greater emphasis on the journal relative to the ledger in some European countries. Vance ("The Authority of History in Inventory Valuation," *The Accounting Review*, July 1943, pp. 219-227) provides another example of the attempt to relate a particular idea or practice to the place, period, and circumstances of its origin or development.

Warrantedness of Accounting Propositions

Our survey in this first chapter of the syllabus is intended to introduce the student to sources of historical materials on accounting, and to isolate a few questions on the basis of their connection with the issue of warrantedness of accounting propositions. These questions revolve around the conceptions of "evolution" of accounting practice, and "causation" as compared to concomitance. The issue may be presented this way: with respect to two events selected by you as having occurred in a time order (that is, one event occurred first), on what ground can you validly assert that one event was the result of the other, or that the first event "caused" the second?

In the study assignments you are referred to portions of Littleton's book (*Accounting Evolution to 1900*) that seem most germane to the evolutionary idea suggested by the book's title. Current literature abounds with references to "evolutionary development" as justification for current practices. What weight are you inclined to give to the proposition that current accounting practice is sound because it is the consequence of a (slow) evolutionary development?

The Accounting Principles Board, an agency of the American Institute of Certified Public Accountants, has accepted as an aim the reduction of variety in practice. Without now considering the suitability of an "authoritative" approach to the development of accounting principles, how can one reconcile the idea of concerted effort to reduce diversity of accounting practice with the idea that current practices are sound because they must be assumed to meet business needs (or because they reflect "evolutionary development," or should be regarded as sound because they exist)?

The term "evolution" sets up a broad environmental picture. The theory of biologic evolution includes the notion of "give-and-take," or mutual adaptation of species with their environment, including other species as components of the environment. Merely casual reflection will suggest that Man has substantially influenced environmental conditions by deliberate, purposeful conduct. Is the element of organized action a component of the doctrine of "accounting evolution" as propounded in Littleton's book? Is it a component of the current argument that existing accounting practices are sound because they are the result of a slow, evolutionary development? Is there a concept of *First Cause* implicit in the doctrine of accounting evolution as used in contemporary argumentation?

An Accounting Classic

Chapter 1 of the Littleton book is recommended reading. It is an accounting classic, by Henry Rand Hatfield, titled "An Historical Defense of Bookkeeping." This essay was written in an academic environment in which accounting was regarded as a brash outsider. Hatfield's purpose was to justify accounting as part of a university curriculum.

READINGS[1]

LITTLETON, A. C., *Accounting Evolution to 1900*
 Study: Preface; pp. 12-21 on "antecedents of double-entry bookkeeping"; pp. 361-368 on "accounting evolution."
 Scan: Chapter 5 on Paciolo's text.

TAYLOR, R. EMMETT, "Luca Pacioli," in *Studies in the History of Accounting*, ed. A. C. Littleton and B. S. Yamey, pp. 175-184.

YAMEY, B. S., "Introduction," in *Studies in the History of Accounting*, ed. A. C. Littleton and B. S. Yamey, pp. 1-13.

YAMEY, B. S., "Scientific Bookkeeping and the Rise of Capitalism," in *Studies in Accounting*, ed. W. T. Baxter, pp. 13-30.

EDEY, H. C., AND PROT PANITPAKDI, "British Company Accounting and the Law 1844-1900," in *Studies in the History of Accounting*, ed. A. C. Littleton and B. S. Yamey, pp. 356-379.

---

[1] Complete book references are given in the Bibliography at the end of the book.

QUESTIONS

1. Will the bases, grounds, or criteria selected by you to constitute the history of accounting include "nonaccounting" events?

2. Why did your history begin as it did? Why did it not begin with earlier or later events? Was your choice of a beginning, as well as your choice of subsequent events, controlled by an idea of a *terminal point* with respect to which the selected events were regarded as means to the attainment of the situation identified as the terminal point? If not, on what other grounds was your selection of events made to constitute the "history"?

3. What, in your view, is Littleton's meaning of "evolution" and of "long evolutionary struggle"? How does that meaning compare with biologic evolution? What evidence do you see for an evolution of accountancy?

4. Did Littleton trace sequences of events that terminated in the employment of a methodology called double-entry bookkeeping? Is an explanation of the development of double-entry bookkeeping given in the remainder of Littleton's book, for which Chapter 2 on "The Antecedents of Double-Entry Bookkeeping" is a preliminary statement of a thesis?

5. What are some characteristics of Littleton's writing which are important for evaluating his statements? Does he typically hypostatize? Does the support for his statements rest more on assertions about origins or on a tracing of probable consequences? When he refers to double-entry bookkeeping as a "complete and unified methodology" is he referring to more than a set of procedures? Does Littleton identify theory with discourse? Does Littleton expressly include experiment as an element in the establishment of a theory?

6. Does a concept of "causation" underlie Littleton's exposition? Is it his view that ends are fixed "in the nature of things," and that the course of development of bookkeeping, as of everything else, is determined by an originally created pattern, attributed to a *First Cause?* (Look up the dictionary meaning of "teleology.")

7. Elsewhere in his book Littleton distinguishes the "form" from the "substance" of double-entry bookkeeping. Do you characteristically contrast form and substance? Do you share the classic Greek view that phenomena which you experience provide incomplete knowledge, and that the process of acquiring knowledge con-

sists in elicitation of the universal character manifested in changing forms?

8. Did double-entry bookkeeping have a "beginning" in Roman times or in the medieval period? Can this decision be made by "tracing the origin"? Or is the "origin" itself a conclusion that is based on the selection of events as relevant? Is the Roman practice regarding debt records relevant in this connection? Do the opinions of Yamey and of Littleton coincide or diverge on the latter point?

9. Assuming that a reading of historic records shows that double-entry bookkeeping was first used, with modifications in detail, in various parts of Italy at about the same time, in what way does this fact discredit the hypothesis that double-entry bookkeeping was invented by a single genius?

10. On what general grounds can the *Zeitgeist* theory of the origin of double-entry bookkeeping be criticized? On the ground of internal inconsistency between painstaking operations associated with the double-entry method and the characteristics, such as "breadth and simplicity" which define the meaning of *Zeitgeist?* On the ground that an alternative and simpler explanation is available for the phenomenon of double-entry bookkeeping?

11. Are the currently employed rules for income determination and asset valuation "logically necessary" in the sense that they are implied by double-entry bookkeeping? Or are other valuation rules also not inconsistent with the double-entry scheme?

12. What considerations should determine the selection of income-determination and asset-valuation rules? What influences did in fact determine the present pattern of accounting-treatment rules? How important, in the explanation, is the public demand for protection against maneuvers by self-seeking managements? Did the conventions arise primarily as the manifestation of a balancing of equities or as an expert expression of the functional relationships between resources and product?

13. Has the crystallization of accounting-treatment rules into standards of practice obstructed a process of adaptation of rules to changed circumstances? Is the basic accounting problem one of the existence of standards or of the relation of standards to business and social needs? How have the circumstances of business practice changed between 1850 and today?

14. What is the general character of Yamey's argument against Sombart's thesis that Western capitalism was importantly influenced by double-entry bookkeeping? Did Yamey simply assert

that a case had not been made for the thesis? Did he use personalities or occupation arguments to influence readers' attitudes toward the authors? Did he treat the matter as an intellectual problem? Did Yamey agree on the specification of "capitalism"?

15. Could Yamey have put the above matter to a laboratory test? If not, could he nevertheless apply the principle of the experimental method? Did he relate implied consequences of the Sombart argument to independently established data which were regarded as facts? If double-entry bookkeeping were vital to successful business practice, one would expect to find double-entry prevalent in business practice. What does the evidence of business records show on the use of double-entry bookkeeping during the period in question?

16. Did Yamey also begin with facts used in the demonstration of the Sombart thesis and suggest alternative theories, hypotheses, or explanations for the accepted phenomena? Accepting as a fact that double-entry bookkeeping was used in some cases, what explanations were suggested as a sufficient condition for the use of that technique? Can the observed extension of double-entry bookkeeping be adequately explained in terms of its utility for keeping track of debtor-creditor dealings and for providing a comprehensive view of financial elements of the business? Can venture-accounting be explained in terms of a need for the physical control of merchandise?

17. Did Yamey question the reasonableness or realism of basic premises in the Sombart argument? Was there implicit agreement between the Yamey and Sombart positions in the postulation of an innovating businessman who is guided by "rational" calculations of value-cost relations?

18. Was the logical necessity of the Sombart argument questioned by Yamey? While agreeing with the premise of a "rational," profit-calculating businessman, did Yamey suggest that the calculation could have been effected informally, on the basis of information developed through the businessman's intimate contact with the operations of his business; and that double-entry bookkeeping was a *sufficient* condition but not a *necessary* condition for the rise of a profit economy?

19. Did Yamey also point to errors in the deductive elaboration of the Sombart argument? If current decisions were to be guided by past records of costs and profits, then the circumstances of past transactions would need to be represented in the future

anticipations. Yamey took it to be a fact, however, that the several ventures were more diverse than similar in respect to factors influencing profit.

20. Do the English Company Acts prior to the twentieth century indicate a major concern for profit measurement or for asset and liability presentation? Was the creditor interest paramount in the shaping of laws regulating dividend payments? That is, was the legislation concerned with assuring that a *minimum* excess of assets over liabilities was a condition for dividend distribution? Was asset valuation controlled by its function in implementing the dividend statutes?

21. In what ways may English Company Accounting have influenced accounting in the United States?

2

An Historical Approach
to Accounting Illustrated
with Events since 1900

In 1940 the American Accounting Association published a monograph by W. A. Paton and A. C. Littleton, called *An Introduction to Corporate Accounting Standards*. This monograph has since become remarkably popular. It is an attempt to outline the "basic theory" which justifies the set of propositions titled "A Tentative Statement of Accounting Principles Underlying Corporate Financial Statements," published in *The Accounting Review* for June, 1936. The 1936 statement and the 1940 monograph represent the first organized effort to formulate a coordinated body of propositions as a reference base for accounting practices in a wide domain.

The foreword to the Paton and Littleton monograph, written by Howard C. Greer, refers to an accounting development which was "rapidly accelerated during the past two decades." The two decades would seem to cover the period between the two World Wars. Even before World War I significant changes had occurred in technology, in business and economic organization for production and distribution, and in financial institutions, the importance of which for accounting was to be recognized more fully later.

Objective of the Chapter

The objective of the present chapter of this syllabus is to examine events significant for accounting for a limited period prior to the Second World War, in order to provide a background for the dynamic accounting thought of the subsequent period and for modern critical attempts to formulate an "accounting theory." Our major interest is in accounting practice and accounting thought, but these cannot be appreciated in isolation. The events examined

9

by a historian for their narrative significance can be as diverse as human and physical activity, but are typically limited by his point of view.

The Historical Premise

The historical premise is that events are interactions; the latter have both antecedents and consequences. The more influential of the events are brought forward against a backdrop of the conditioning environment. Further perspective may be developed by advancing certain of the characteristic events, say the "accounting events," toward the lens position, while leaving the other factors in the background as a conditioning flux.

What events of the period since 1900 do you think influenced the condition of accounting at the time of the beginning of the organized search for accounting principles? And what characteristics do you select to represent the condition of accounting? Is your selection made at random, by "intuition," or is it guided by some controlling conceptions about interactions? Do you assume that investors are controlled or guided by publicly reported net income figures? That businessmen are motivated to maximize profits? That expressed governmental authority will be obeyed, or evaded where conformance would reduce profits? That economic conduct is always rational or may enter into phases suggested by the terms "inflation," "deflation," and "depression"? That accounting practices entering into public reporting are adopted independently of federal income tax privileges or are substantially influenced by the federal income tax laws?

Illustration of an Accounting Narrative

Narration of a historical background for accounting developments may be illustrated as follows:

By the turn of the century the era of mergers and combinations had already been recognized. Relatively small business operations, typically controlled by a small financial and ownership nucleus, had coalesced into large aggregates characterized by professional management and absentee stockholders. The management desire for control data was bolstered by the need to supply investors periodically with significant financial information. Financial reporting was further complicated by the fact of intercorporate holdings.

More adequate record-keeping was forced upon smaller businesses by the Income Tax Act of 1913 and subsequent revenue laws.

It is possible that the outstanding influence of World War I on accounting thought was through the concomitant price inflation. By 1921 stocks of commodities had advanced appreciably in price, and the characteristic first-in-first-out (FIFO) method of pricing inventory had placed the appreciation in the preceding income statements and in earned surplus. The collapse of prices in 1921 gave rise subsequently to charges that FIFO inventory pricing resulted in "fools' profits." More generally, accounting was criticized for failing to reflect the real facts of economic life.

The return to "normalcy" was accompanied by speculative fever and the creation of super-holding companies and an emphasis in accounting on consolidated financial statements. In many instances the speculative increases in asset values associated with stock-price increases were brought into the net worth accounts of the corporations, and into the income statements through increased depreciation charges. The problem of the treatment of plant appreciation gained in importance.

The stock market crash of 1929 ushered in a period of economic depression. Asset values and income measures fell to new lows that seemed self-reinforcing. Previous write-ups were erased and additional losses were recognized in the accounts on revaluation of assets. The political climate favored investor safeguards, and securities legislation was introduced along with a gamut of economic-aid devices. Among the latter was the National Industrial Recovery Act (NIRA) technique of tied-in costs and prices, and industry compulsion on the individual producer and businessman.

During the period from 1933 to 1939 slow economic recovery was either facilitated or retarded by new legislative policies and increased administrative direction of business by government. The Securities and Exchange Commission adopted a policy of stimulating the accounting profession to regulate itself. It is at the end of this period that the Accounting Procedure Committee of the American Institute of Accountants instituted its series of Accounting Research Bulletins.

Significant changes in income tax rules occurred during the latter period. Under U.S. Treasury policy, depreciation deductions were closely scrutinized and the burden of proving deductions for depreciation was in effect placed on the taxpayers. In 1938 last-in-first-out (LIFO) inventory valuation was permitted for limited classes of taxpayers, and in 1939 the LIFO privilege was generalized for taxpayers.

In other countries price inflation had in some instances run away with the economy. In the United States the professional interest in accounting for capital and income during a period of rapid price inflation was represented in the publications of Sweeney and some others on what Sweeney called "stabilized accounting."

Interests and Purpose of the Researcher

Other historical facts and relationships can, of course, be brought into the background structure. A description of social attitudes may help to explain taxing measures. The banking structure and the dominance of the creditor-protection interest may be developed as contributing to an understanding of the practices of the time. Other practices may best be viewed as vestiges of Italian precepts or medieval requirements, and the historical narration may extend into the distant past. The clarion of freedom and the capitalistic system has sometimes been sounded for proper appreciation of the tones of double-entry methodology.

What is background and what is the center of consideration will vary with the interests and purpose of the researcher. He may concentrate on the perennial problem of depreciation accounting. His attention may be directed to the issue of Cash Basis versus Accrual Basis accounting. The issue of inventory valuation gained prominence with the aftermath of World War I and again with the permissive use of LIFO for the federal income tax. LIFO valuation was emphasized also with the development of national income statistics. Plant asset write-ups and write-downs and associated amortization problems arose out of the extensive price movements of the 1920's and the 1930's.

Or the researcher may be interested in the more general phenomenon of income reporting. What influences enter into an explanation of the observed shift in emphasis on income reporting and position reporting? It is unlikely that the student will ignore the passage of federal securities legislation and the creation of the Securities and Exchange Commission. A concomitant of this development was the beginning of organized search into the more fundamental bases of accounting methodology.

With the Securities and Exchange Commission's emphasis on investor protection through adequate disclosure of relevant financial information, more intensive consideration was given to the functions of the *Balance Sheet* and the *Income Statement*. The relatively greater attention accorded the Income Statement in published reports and in the literature of the period was associated with a rising interest in stockholder-investor protection. The residuum character of the Balance Sheet was to receive greater prominence later, with the widespread adoption of LIFO valuation of inventories and with price-level changes.

Association Contrasted with Explanation

But an association of events and conditions, as exhibited in a historical narrative, is not a sufficient *explanation*. The completed exposition may be regarded as a hypothesis, susceptible to only partial verification. It reflects the narrator's conceptions about mutual influences or interactions. And its pattern is determined by the researcher's picture of the terminated situation with respect to which the selected events are regarded as conditioning factors. This is to say that a history is dependent, for its public or relatively objective character, upon agreement at many points, on the quality of the situation which is to be regarded as the close or termination of influences, and on types of interactions which make the selected events relevant in a means-consequences relation.

The Nagel and Dewey study assignments present some general issues regarding historical judgments. The Brundage article presents an accounting history.

Accounting Education

A special interest of the graduate student may motivate him to give special attention to the influence of accounting education on accounting practice. This interest may develop the search almost into an activity for its own sake, beginning with a study of early schools of accounting and extending to an analysis of present and projected curricula in accounting. What appear at first glance to be new ideas may be traced to earlier roots or comparable plants, as in Nissley, "Education for the Profession of Accounting" (*Journal of Accountancy*, August 1935, pp. 90-103). A still earlier article (Jackson, "Present Tendencies in Business Education," *Journal of Accountancy*, November 1927, pp. 346-359) has a remarkably modern flavor in its emphasis away from vocational training and toward education for a career. The notion of a separate professional school recurs in the literature, evidencing an ancestry for the corresponding topic included in a recent convention program of the American Accounting Association.

READINGS

NAGEL, ERNEST, *The Structure of Science,* pp. 568-575 on "explanations of aggregative events."

DEWEY, JOHN, *Logic, The Theory of Inquiry,* pp. 220, 230-239, on historical judgments.

BRUNDAGE, PERCIVAL F., "Milestones on the Path of Accounting," *Harvard Business Review,* July 1951, pp. 71-81.

QUESTIONS

1. One modern accounting textbook calls accounting a "branch of history." Does this viewpoint rule out reference to future events?

2. Is an accounting historian a "theorist"? Can past events be explained without reference to conceptions about interactions? Can present practices be understood without reference to past events and conditions? Is the quest for understanding present accounting practices equivalent to the search for theories?

3. We saw that several, alternative, theories of the origin of double-entry bookkeeping were extant for long periods of time. How is this fact related to processes of verification of theories? Can

you distinguish "capability of verification" from "verifiability in principle"? Would you regard all statements that did not meet the latter test as "nonsense"?

4. What reasons can you think of, in addition to new discoveries of relevant data, why histories need to be reformulated? Do philosophical predispositions influence the character of a history? Does the historian's conception about the termination of events, or the "end in view," regulate the selection of data as elements in the narrative?

5. Can conceptions about terminating conditions vary among historians? May such conceptions be influenced by the culture of the period of the historian's existence? Have the standards of financial reporting since 1900 exhibited a progressive improvement? How is the shift in emphasis from the Balance Sheet to the Income Statement accommodated in your history of financial-reporting standards?

6. Does accounting state events "as they actually happened"? Does the preparation of an Income Statement involve a selection among past events? How is the selection of events controlled? Do the principles of selection-control take into account possible future events? If so, is that fact characteristic of histories? Do your answers to the preceding questions carry any implications for the interpretation of "historical cost"?

7. What is the apparent purpose of the writer in the Brundage article on "Milestones"? Is this article a history of accounting during the first half of the twentieth century? Does the author attempt to explain particular occurrences? Collective events? Does the explanation follow a *genetic* pattern?

8. Did Brundage regard accounting as one of the "social forces" whose interaction determined a change from position R_s to position R_t? Or was accounting regarded as a neutral or passive element, changes in which were consequences of interactions among (other) social forces but which was not a force itself in shaping business "developments"?

9. Did Brundage regard the U. S. Steel merger in 1901 as a "precipitating" event that upset an "equilibrium" under which social forces impinging on business had effected a stationary state for accounting? Was the Hepburn amendment to the Interstate Commerce Act an aggravating event in the same line of change that had been instituted by the U. S. Steel merger, or had another equilib-

rium position been reached prior to a second "precipitating" event? Had other equilibrium positions been attained just before the outbreak of World War I? 1930? 1939? 1949?

10. What generalizations did Brundage use to represent the manner in which "accounting" was influenced by the "milestone" events? Or were the "milestones" merely points at which the consequences of continuous influences on accounting were noticeable? On the first interpretation, what was the assumed mode of influence of the federal income tax on depreciation accounting after 1913? What assumptions about human behavior are used in that analysis? Are those assumptions "probabilistic" as contrasted with "universal" propositions?

11. What generalizations would you use to explain the influence of depreciation rules introduced by the Internal Revenue Code of 1954 on corporate financial accounting? In other words, how do you connect the particular occurrence of Section 167 of the Internal Revenue Code with the extended use of accelerated depreciation for corporate financial reporting? Is the connection sufficiently established through the words "led to," or "caused," or "contributed to"?

3

A Problem Situation
for Professional Accountants
and Structures
for Organized Accounting Research

It is one of the purposes of the reading assignments to present a problem situation facing the accounting profession in the 1930s. An ideological aspect of prior developments is interestingly told by Nelson ("Science and Accounting," *The Accounting Review*, October 1949, pp. 354-359), who refers to "the exigencies of a 'later altered situation' with which accounting has been confronted since 1930."

The Securities and Exchange Commission had not enforced its directive to the Chief Accountant to draft a prescription for accounting practices, and the accounting fraternity was being challenged to demonstrate the order that it asserted underlay corporate financial statements. Sanders, Hatfield, and Moore (*A Statement of Accounting Principles*) had accepted a charge to present an organized statement of the rules guiding accounting practices. The American Institute of Accountants reconstituted and vitalized a committee which undertook to state its opinions on selected accounting matters. A committee of the American Accounting Association in 1936 published a statement of "principles" to serve as guides in constructing financial statements for the large industrial corporation. Impatience with traditional accounting rules is reflected in the vigorous expression by MacNeal, assigned for study. It appeared that accounting, in the institutional sense, was on the move.

Character of Organized Accounting Research in the United States

Our consideration of the continuous sponsorship of accounting research in the United States can be limited to a few organizations. The influence of the New York Stock Exchange and of the Securities and Exchange Commission on accounting research has been largely indirect. Financial grants by foundations have facilitated individual research projects, including the Sanders-Hatfield-Moore *Statement of Accounting Principles*. Our present interest is in recurring products of research associated with the American Accounting Association, the American Institute of Certified Public Accountants, the National Accounting Association, and the Controllers Institute Research Foundation. Insight into the research objectives of the latter two organizations may be obtained from their publications and from official accounts appearing in *The Accounting Review* for January, 1961. The following statements relate to research products of the pertinent committees of the American Accounting Association and the American Institute of Certified Public Accountants. For convenience in exposition, reference will generally be made to the organization names rather than to the committee titles. The organizations will sometimes be designated AAA and AICPA, respectively.

A Major Research Effort of the AAA: Accounting and Reporting Standards for Corporate Financial Statements

In 1936, after about four years of concrete planning, the American Accounting Association published *A Tentative Statement of Accounting Principles Affecting Corporate Reports*. That document has passed through several revisions and supplementation. The most recent comparable Statement was promulgated in 1957 under the title *Accounting and Reporting Standards for Corporate Financial Statements, 1957 Revision*. The entire set of statements and supplements through 1957 is available under a single cover from the Association.

The 1936 Statement evoked considerable comment. A belief

that acceptance of the standards represented in the 1936 Statement must be founded on understanding was evidenced by the preparation and publication in 1940 of an exposition of "the basic theory which underlies the Tentative Statement." The title of the American Accounting Association monograph was *An Introduction to Corporate Accounting Standards*. The authors, W. A. Paton and A. C. Littleton, were influential teachers and were prominent in the field of accounting literature. Subsequent statements of standards were expected to be controlled by "the fundamental ideas of accounting" presented in the monograph, according to the preface by the authors.

The Contemporary Research Effort of the AICPA: Postulates, Principles, Inventory, and Codification

The early approach to accounting research by the American Institute of Accountants was particularistic. Prior to 1938 an Accounting Procedure Committee was "available" to answer questions of proper persons about appropriate accounting treatments. During the preceding several years more centrally directed efforts had been made to effect agreement with the Securities and Exchange Commission on the source of accounting standards. Publication of Accounting Series Release (ASR) No. 4 in 1938 marked acceptance, by the Securities and Exchange Commission, of a crucial proposition: that the appropriateness of a particular accounting treatment rested on the conclusion that the practice had "substantial authoritative support."

The Accounting Procedure Committee was reconstituted in 1938. The committee's demise occurred in 1959, 21 years after its creation. The membership of the committee at any one time was 21 persons. Each person was appointed for a term of one year. Whatever continuity of research effort developed had to come from the small nucleus of technical research staff. The latter group was small in number at the outset and declined in number over the years. Considerable continuity of *viewpoint* existed, however, through the preponderance of practicing certified public accountants, including representatives of the large firms, in the membership of the committee. The committee's preoccupation with problems of practice imparted a general character to its several "pronouncements" on accounting treatments, issued as Accounting Research Bulletins. Selection of topics for deliberation was on an ad hoc basis. Statements of considerations underlying conclusions about appropriate treatments were sparse.

Despite the limited scope of research effort underlying the committee's conclusions, the committee's activities may be deemed successful when related to the committee's apparent objectives. The American Institute of Accountants had provided an influential body of persons (apart from their committee status) to serve as an organ of communication with the New York Stock Exchange and with the Securities and Exchange Commission. The committee was readily available to consider "hot" issues, and to represent the Institute's viewpoint that the source of accounting standards was the accounting profession. Positions taken by the committee and published in the Bulletins presumably reflected a practical balancing of interests. More importantly, publication of the Bulletins implemented the principle of "substantial authoritative support," accepted by the Securities and Exchange Commission in ASR No. 4. The quality of "substantial authoritative support" was imparted to a particular accounting treatment by the Mikadoian device of saying "let a thing be done . . ." The force of the conclusion was judged by the stature of the body that uttered it.

By 1958 the influence of the Accounting Procedure Committee in shaping "generally accepted accounting principles" had become widely recognized. The relative participation of practicing certified public accountants in the process, as compared to controllers and accounting teachers, was a source of dissatisfaction. So also was the manner in which the committee reached its conclusions, with relatively little research effort and independently of any guiding structure of ideas, or at least without explicit reference to any controlling "theory." A progressive President appointed a special committee in 1958 to study the research effort of the Institute.

The recommendations of the special study committee were accepted by the Council of the Institute in 1959. The old Accounting Procedure Committee was discontinued. A new Accounting Principles Board was created, and the relative representation of full-time practicing certified public accountants was reduced. Larger representation was given to the groups of corporate officials and university and college teachers. The philosophy for the new structure included a fuller exploration of considerations appropriate to the choice of particular standards, and the formation of judgments by reference to a body of propositions constituting an accounting theory.

In a later chapter of this syllabus we shall examine the results of the research studies, published as Accounting Research Study No. 1 and Accounting Research Study No. 3, which were proposed to the Accounting Principles Board for adoption as postulates and principles to which subsequent determinations on specific issues would be related.

The recommendations of the two Accounting Research Studies were rejected by the Accounting Principles Board in 1962. Current research sponsored by the Institute is in the direction of inventorying and codifying "generally accepted accounting principles."

Chapters 6 through 9 of this syllabus examine the main threads of accounting-standards formulation which may be traced, on the one hand, through the 1936 Statement of the American Accounting Association committee and the related monograph of Paton and Littleton, and on the other hand, to comparatively recent research developments associated with the American Institute of Certified Public Accountants' establishment of the Accounting Principles Board. On what bases can the student appraise the products of these organized efforts? What criteria can be applied to judge their soundness or their fruitfulness? What tests of validity need to be applied to the propositions which assert that some ways of treating financial data are preferred to others, for use by management or for incorporation in published financial reports?

In Chapter 4 of this syllabus the student will have the opportunity to refresh his memory on, or be introduced to, certain matters in philosophy which are directly relevant to the question of the conditions that a proposition must satisfy in order to be acceptable. Attention is then transferred from the general problem of warrantability of propositions to accounting contexts in which the issue has recently been presented.

READINGS

MAY, GEORGE O., *Twenty-Five Years of Accounting Responsibility.*
Correspondence between the Special Committee on Cooperation with Stock Exchanges of the American Institute of Accountants and the Committee on Stock List of the New York
Stock Exchange, Vol. 1, pp. 112-144.

SANDERS, T. H., HENRY HATFIELD, AND UNDERHILL MOORE, *A Statement of Accounting Principles.* Study the letter of transmittal,
and the summary on pp. 113-116.

MACNEAL, KENNETH, "What's Wrong with Accounting?", in *Studies
in Accounting Theory,* ed. W. T. Baxter and Sidney Davidson,
pp. 56-69.

QUESTIONS

1. In selecting a beginning position for the purpose of *explaining* the modern development of accounting principles or
standards, what considerations would lead you to select one or
another of the following alternative dates and occurrences: (a)
institution of the Committee on Accounting Procedure of the
American Institute of Accountants in 1939; (b) passage of the federal securities legislation in 1933 and 1934; (c) cooperative activities of the American Institute of Accountants and the New York
Stock Exchange as exemplified in correspondence reproduced in the
assigned reading in May's book; (d) widespread reaction to Ripley's article criticizing corporate financial reporting of the time,
which included a suggestion that the Federal Trade Commission
enter into the determination of acceptable accounting standards;
(e) the depression of 1893 and the "sound money policy" adopted
in 1896; (f) some earlier occurrence, such as the Kreuger events depicted in nonassigned portions of May's book?

2. Accounting historians have asserted that a shift in emphasis occurred from the Balance Sheet to the Income Statement.
Does Mr. May's letter of September 22, 1932, to the Committee on
Stock List of the New York Stock Exchange indicate that the relative emphasis was on the Income Statement at that time? Could a
corresponding deemphasis on the Balance Sheet be regarded as a
means of shunting some of the force of current criticism that the
position statement did not in fact represent current values? Would
such an interpretation be fair?

3. From the standpoint of positive explanation of Income-Statement emphasis, it has been said that the principal function of that statement is to exhibit "earning capacity" or "earning power." (For example, Mr. May's letter of September 22, 1932, referred to "earning capacity.") Are the terms "capacity" and "power" synonymous in this connection? Or should a choice between the two terms depend on one's viewpoint toward the reflection of estimates in the financial statements?

4. Mr. May limited the application of the phrase "earning capacity" to the specified time period with which Income-Statement data were associated. Does the identification of earning capacity require the specification of all the major environmental and operating factors, including market conditions, associated with the identified revenue for the period elapsed? Even if attention is limited to financial aspects of operating conditions, does the reference to "capacity" (or "power") suggest the relevance of resources, and the focusing of attention on the Balance Sheet?

5. In what sense do Income-Statement data show earning "capacity"? Does your explanation on the latter point involve estimates of future events?

6. How do you reconcile the following statements? (a) Asset values depend on earning prospects. (b) The calculation of net earnings must take asset consumption into account.

7. Under the proposal of the Institute's Committee on Co-operation with Stock Exchanges as contained in Mr. May's letter of September 22, 1932, was the adequacy of affected corporate financial statements referrable to (a) "generally accepted accounting principles"; (b) standard practice within the industry; or (c) principles of treatment selected by each company for its own reports and presented to the stock exchange for purposes of reference?

8. If the accounting-treatment rules in fact employed by a particular corporation were known to investors, would the report of an independent public accountant that the specified procedures had been consistently applied by that corporation meet the standard of "full disclosure"? Does the position just stated reflect the views of the May committee in 1932? Or did that committee's proposal to the New York Stock Exchange Committee on Stock List restrict the choices of accounting-treatment rules available to the listed corporations?

9. What, in your opinion, is the most basic constraint that the May committee would have had the stock exchanges impose on the financial reporting of listed corporations? Can this constraint

be summarily expressed as "the realization convention"? Or as "the doctrine of historical cost"? Do these two expressions amount to the same thing?

10.   What do you infer to be the meaning of "fairly present" as adopted by the Governing Committee of the New York Stock Exchange through its Resolution of October 25, 1933? Was this term either different from, or broader than, the "fair determination" of income in respect to the consistent application of the selected accounting-treatment rules from year to year? Was concordance with the "realization convention" a condition for fair presentation? Was conformity with "accepted accounting practices" a condition for fair presentation?

11. Does the reading of the May correspondence indicate specifications for "accepted accounting practices"? Was one specification that the practice have the support of "substantial authority"?

12. What do you infer to be the meaning of "fairly present" advocated by certain major accounting firms in the correspondence assigned for study in this syllabus? Was the emphasis on "conservatism" in the sense of avoidance of overstatement of income? Was a "conservative" result expected from the application of the "realization convention" during an extended period of economic growth and moderate price inflation? Was the phrase "correctness of balance sheets" to be interpreted by reference to economic values or by reference to the results of applying the historical-cost standard? Did the accounting viewpoint at that time provide additional flexibility to management through the "good faith" doctrine?

13. According to the current meaning of "fairly present" as used in the accountants' opinion, does the term "fairly present" have an independent meaning apart from the adjective "in accordance with generally accepted principles of accounting . . ."? Or is "fairly present" defined by reference to the application of those specific procedures which in the aggregate constitute "generally accepted principles of accounting"?

14. Is fairness an "inherent property" of certain accounting rules, such that the "possession" of this "property" will constitute a rule a principle? Is "fairness" a judgment applied to a practice in respect to the anticipated consequences of its application? Is inquiry into "nature" or into "consequences" likely to be more productive for the development of accounting standards?

15. The Securities and Exchange Commission received authority from Congress to prescribe accounting-treatment rules for corporations under the jurisdiction of the Commission. That power

was applied "judiciously" and "with restraint," according to George O. May (*Financial Accounting*, 1961 revision, p. 66). As a condition for the deferment of the Commission's exercise of its power to prescribe accounting-treatment rules, the American Institute of Accountants faced the practical requirement of specifying "accepted accounting principles." The apparent sanction that accounting practice gave to alternative accounting-treatment rules in identical situations helped to shape the form of the problem as one of reducing diversity. Stated differently, the problem was one of "standardizing" accounting practices or of achieving greater "uniformity" of accounting standards. In what sense is the term "uniformity" used in this connection?

16. In 1935 Haskins & Sells Foundation, Inc., invited three well-known accountants to "formulate a code of accounting principles," which it compared with codifications of civil and criminal laws. The verbalized objective was either the creation (evolution) or the identification of a workable number of guiding principles to which practices could be related. That the purpose was the creative development of principles rather than merely their selection and identification was suggested by the stated hope that the product of the committee's efforts would "attain to" acceptance on a broad scale.

The study was completed in 1937. From the authors' letter of transmittal, what is your interpretation of their own views about their objective? Did they view their function as that of codification of accounting opinion on what are the appropriate accounting standards or as a creative development of principles of sound treatment?

17. In what manner were the "principles" identified by Sanders, Hatfield, and Moore intended to control practice? In the sense that acceptable practices were deductively related to the stated "principles"? Or in the sense that "principles" specified conditions under which specified kinds of actions and associated consequences were expected?

18. Is the term "hypostatization" correctly applied to the assignment of personal qualities to abstractions? Does the term apply to the statement that principles "dictate"? Or that principles "permit" or "forbid" various lines of activity? Or do the latter terms relate merely to verbal characteristics of statements in which certain rules are specified? Under the latter interpretation how are "principles" distinguished from other "rules"? How would you characterize the "principles" "stated" by Sanders, Hatfield, and Moore?

19. The Sanders, Hatfield, and Moore Statement concludes that the "existence" of a "body of generally accepted accounting principles" is a fact; and it cites as evidence the reference which the accountants' "certificate" makes to "accepted principles of accounting." Does this conclusion agree with that of the May committee in 1932? Was the plan proposed by the May committee that *each* corporation should specify the rules which *it* used, subject only to acceptance of not more than six "broad principles" including the realization doctrine? Did May relate the phrase "in accordance with accepted principles of accounting" to the small number of "broad principles" variously implemented by other rules that the particular corporation acknowledged?

20. George O. May's committee in 1932 had told the New York Stock Exchange Committee on Stock List that the function of the balance sheet should *not* be regarded as presenting values at a point in time. May was responding partly to Ripley's premise in *Main Street and Wall Street*. In 1939 MacNeal adopted the proposition that the balance sheet should portray economic values and extended it to include the idea that accountants intended that the balance sheet should convey the impression that it did represent economic values, at least prior to 1933. MacNeal's evidence for the latter position was a dictionary meaning of "correct," a critical word used in the accountants' certificate. Following Federal Trade Commission reaction to the use of the word "correct," the accountants' certificate was changed to encompass the phrase "fairly present." Did MacNeal feel that a "fair" showing was provided by adherence to the accounting conventions in fact employed by corporations, and which were reviewed by accountants? Can you assess MacNeal's argument on "going-concern-value theory"?

4

Conditions for Knowledge
and the Activity of Knowing:
A Reference Standard for Accounting

In Chapter 1 some representative views on accounting changes up to 1900 were noted, and inquiry was made into the meaning of evolutionary development. In Chapter 2 some problems of the historical method were observed through its application to accounting developments since 1900. The character of subsequent organized accounting research structures was sketched in association with an introduction to a continuing problem situation for professional accountants, in Chapter 3.

In the present chapter emphasis is placed on identification of conditions for assertibility of statements generally, and subsequently, in Chapter 5, on examination of conditions for assertibility of statements in the field of accounting. The purpose of Chapter 4 is to help the reader to begin to build a background in strains of philosophic thought as a condition for understanding and appraising that portion of accounting literature which attempts to justify a particular selection from among alternative accounting-treatment rules.

The Interpretation Problem

What do we know? How do we know it? Are the knowns recognized intuitively? Are intuitive "truths" added to by the operation of an innate mental faculty, through a process of "ratiocination"? Is knowledge built up, in building-block form, by deductions from fundamental propositions that are intuitively recognized as true? Is axiomatization of fields of inquiry the urgent need of the twentieth century? Is there room for debate on criteria for selecting the axioms and for choosing operating and transformation rules?

Or is observation the key to knowledge? Does the construction of theories begin with the apprehension of simple ideas that are images of the observed "physical" world? If perceptions are the building blocks of knowledge, what evidence is there of natural-world facts as "causes" of the percepts? Is there a mind that perceives, set off from the world which is perceived? May the source of percepts be a greater Mind, rather than an external world of physical objects?

And how is all of this related to accounting?

It will become evident from the later assigned readings that accounting writers are searching for explanations of practices and justifications for particular doctrines and accounting-treatment rules. They refer to other ideas in support of their positions regarding the doctrines and rules. The references vary from observation, experience, and practice to coherence and clear thinking. Practice is opposed to theory; induction is represented as a process distinct from deduction; the scientific method is identified with an axiomatic approach to knowledge; and practicing accountants return to the certainty that an inventorying of accounting practices may supply.

Within the past ten to fifteen years accounting periodicals have included a number of subtle and sophisticated articles which assume such complicated frames of reference as microeconomic theory, communications theory, the scientific method, or the function of postulates in inquiry. It would seem reasonable to expect graduate accounting students and other inquirers into accounting to understand all classes of articles appearing in accounting periodicals to the extent of having the facility for critically reviewing them. At least a start toward this goal could be made in the undergraduate phase of college education. Placing the entire burden on the introductory section of a single course in the graduate accounting program is unrealistic. But under the view that modern education is a lifetime process, even a late start in examining foundation subjects may be expected to have value.

The Scientific Method

Much has been written about "the scientific method," as a general term for the methodology of science, particularly the physical sciences. Its usefulness in the acquisition of knowledge about the physical world is supported by impressive evidence. A larger difference of opinion exists about the usefulness of the scientific method for exploration in the social "sciences." Salter's book titled *A Critical Review of Research in Land Economics* is of special interest because of its extension of John Dewey's views on the theory of inquiry to an area in the social sciences. A reason for emphasizing Dewey's formulation of logic and its relation to the scientific method is mirrored in the following sentence taken from the concluding chapter (p. 246) of Salter's book: "In John Dewey's work, and particularly in his *Logic,* there is found a modern, functional theory of inquiry, in which misconceptions in older views of scientific method are revealed, and in which the purposes, procedures, and consequences of experimental inquiry are joined into a unified, comprehensive formulation." A discussion of the relation of value considerations to scientific inquiry in the social sciences is presented in the assigned reading in Nagel's *The Structure of Science.*

Whatever the ultimate conclusion about the applicability of the scientific method to areas of social study, the successful use of that method in broad areas of investigation imparts to it a status of a possible condition for acquiring knowledge about other areas with similar problem characteristics. That the scientific method has applications to those areas of human behavior in which the accountant is interested may be regarded as a hypothesis.

Some possible negative value may follow from setting up the standard of the scientific method as a comparison-base for particular inquiries into accounting propositions. Application of the standard should help to disclose the partial and incomplete character of the particular investigation, and to indicate the directions in which additional effort may add to the reliability of the propositions that constituted the close of the partial inquiry. Thus the conditions of scientific inquiry may provide a check-list for identification of operations which can be performed within the limitations of a particular social inquiry. Such a comparison should help to emphasize the tentativeness, if not the unsoundness, of propositions that are the conclusions of the partial inquiry.

Further support for introducing the pattern of the scientific method into the present syllabus is found in the increasing frequency with which the term "scientific method" is used in the literature of accounting standards. Identification of the scientific method in reference to fields in which its use has become accepted is thus a necessary tool of the accounting researcher, for the purpose of evaluating the force of the term in the context in which the term is used by the particular accounting writer. By the aid of this tool the student and the researcher can reduce the danger of letting emotive connotations influence acceptance of propositions with which the term "scientific method" is associated.

Only general statements can be made here about the scientific method. Adequate understanding of this subject is dependent upon extensive study of the historical relations between science and philosophy and upon intensive study of the generalized practices employed successfully in acquiring knowledge of the physical world. You are not asked to accept one particular formulation of the methodology of (physical) science. We assume that you bring some conception of the method of science to the graduate study of accounting. The reading references direct you to statements about the scientific method, and this syllabus highlights Dewey's formulation of that method, for comparison with other approaches to the warrantedness of propositions.

You are asked to employ your concept of the scientific method in analyzing the materials presented in following portions of this syllabus. In this process you should acquire a better appreciation of the difficulties of applying the method of the physical sciences to the social sciences. More particularly, you will have developed a base for recognizing the, often, limited meanings that accounting writers have assigned to the term "scientific method."

Cohen and Nagel on the scientific method

While you are asked to apply your own formulation of the standard of the scientific method to accounting propositions, comparative statements of that method are available to you. Cohen and Nagel (*An Introduction to Logic and Scientific Method*, pp. 197-206) note the following indicators of the scientific method. The beginning of inquiry is the recognition of a problem or unsettled situation. For example, consider Herodotus' query about the reason why the River Nile periodically flowed beyond its channel and inundated the surrounding land. Cohen and Nagel cite the overflowing as a "brute fact" in the absence of a search for the explanation.

These authors say that a statement of the problem is conditioned by some degree of familiarity with the subject-matter.

Several lines of explanation may appear as alternatives. Do the winds from the Mediterranean keep the river water from flowing into the sea? Do melting snows push the water into the river channel at such a rate that it cannot be contained in the channel? Are other suggested explanations worth investigating?

The choice cannot be made simply by "finding the facts of the case." An important part of the problem-solution is the determination of what events or objects are to be regarded *as* facts. This could not be done prior to the suggestion of a particular line of explanation as a possible solution.

The "winds hypothesis" would direct a search to the times when the wind blows off the Mediterranean and the relation of such times to the period of overflow of the Nile. If the wind-flow and water-overflow were coterminous, the winds hypothesis might be further tested by noting whether other rivers under similar wind conditions behaved similarly to the Nile. The directive force of a hypothesis determines what data are possible facts. The "winds hypothesis" of the overflow of the Nile River brought the behavior of other rivers under observation, and that behavior was found by Herodotus to be inconsistent with the winds hypothesis.

The "snow hypothesis" directed attention to the possibility of tall mountains from the direction of the source of the Nile. In the absence of data about such mountains Herodotus relied on inferences from other observed data, selected as facts under the guidance of the snow hypothesis. The Nile River flowed through a hot country, as evidenced by the winds that came from that direction; and the inferred "fact" of a hot country is inconsistent with an assumption of snowfall in that region. The particular connections that Herodotus made between those data which he selected as relevant influenced him to reject also the snow hypothesis.

Exploration further into the interior of Africa, and the discovery of mountain sources of the River Nile would have supported the "snow hypothesis," of course. In addition, the verification of a snow hypothesis for the overflow of the Nile River would have significance for the previously accepted "fact" that there is no snow in the direction from which hot winds blow. In any particular inquiry there is a back-and-forth movement between facts and conceptions. The two aspects of inquiry are interwoven.

An important aspect of the scientific method is the derivation of implications from hypotheses for the purpose of guiding operations that will provide new data suitable for testing the hypothesis. Although a hypothesis may not be subject to direct verification, other aspects of interactions implied by the original hypothesis may be deduced and tested by experimental means. The hypothesis that melting snow accounted for the overflow of the Nile River could not be directly verified in the absence of data about the source of the river. But an implication of the snow hypothesis was taken by Herodotus to be that no winds or cool winds would blow from the direction of the river's source. The latter implication was tested against the observation that hot winds blew from that direction. This illustration should help to emphasize the importance of establishing just what are the postulated interconnections among the data constituting the hypothesis, and on what evidence the elements of the hypothesis are accepted *as* facts for the purpose of the particular inquiry.

Dewey on the scientific method

Dewey (*Logic, The Theory of Inquiry*) identifies logic with conditions that, it has been found, determine whether propositions are "warrantedly assertible," whether in a common-sense or a scientific setting. But appropriate inquiry transforms a common-sense setting into a scientific situation, so that logic may be equated to the conditions for scientific propositions. The characteristic qualities of scientific propositions are that they deal with the classification of things by kinds according to modes of interaction, or they express necessary relations among meanings, and both subtypes of scientific propositions are used to bring some degree of order into an unsettled, or problematic situation. Logical forms are not formalistic, they are functional. They are means for effective inquiry.

Dewey sharply distinguishes existential and conceptual forms, and it may help our understanding to analogize these to a double-lane going down the road of inquiry. In the existential lane, generalizations are made about particulars according to observed modes of interaction; the resulting classes of objects are called "kinds." Dewey's illustrations include lightning, or iron, or dew. One important problem in the existential lane is the determination that a particular thing is, or is not, one of a kind; this process is undertaken by means of comparison-contrast. For example, a piece of ore may need to be identified as either gold or iron pyrites. The objects that constitute a kind are products of operations, and are not a result of psychological perceptions of qualities. Another aspect of inquiry, still in the existential lane, is the determination of relations among kinds, again on the basis of differential consequences. Such a set of relations may be illustrated by types of connections between gaseous, liquid, and solid states of matter, or by the assimilation of lightning with certain other phenomena as electromagnetic events.

In the other lane, corresponding but different operations are performed as phases of inquiry. Meanings are formulated as definitions. In Dewey's example, "all squares are rectangular." Or the conditions of being metallic are set out. Meanings are related in systems, according to modes of operation constituting criteria of transformability. For example, the operations that will be expected to differentiate one metal from another are specified, as well as those operations which provide the ground for differentiating metals from nonmetals and from metalloids. Except for certain possibilities contained *within* mathematics, the relationships of characters are so ordered as to represent existential possibilities. Propositions formulated in a meanings-system are expressed in "if-then" form, and may be designated universal hypothetical propositions. The function of universal propositions is to guide operations in the other, or existential lane in correspondence with the possibilities of interaction suggested by the "if-then" propositions.

In the process of inquiry the two types of propositions are modified in correspondence with each other. Operations performed in correspondence with the controlling conceptions may indicate the need for a different classification of things by "kinds." The earlier assumption that a particular was one of a kind may need to be revised. New combinations of particulars taken to exemplify kinds, which are new combinations precisely because of the mediation of the controlling conceptions or hypotheses, may provide new insights about interactions, and the corresponding meanings-systems and hypotheses will be modified.

The notion that "dew" is a subkind of "rain" was dispelled through institution of operations which were guided by "if-then" propositions concerning heat radiation and conduction. The notion that malaria was causally associated with "bad air" was impotent for instituting operations which, through observation of consequences, could test the "bad air" hypothesis. But a theory of parasitic diseases could suggest a search for carriers, and the previous conclusion that mosquitoes carry *some* diseases could further direct the search. Operations performed with various types of mosquitoes and comparisons with blood cells of malaria sufferers were phases in the development of a hypothesis explaining malaria. In the process malaria was established as a parasitic rather than a bacillic disease.

Dewey's exposition of the scientific method exhibits a high degree of generalization. It does not satisfy a reader's desire for statements of particulars that exemplify the elements and processes hypothetically asserted to constitute inquiry. While the result "makes difficult reading," its reputation for descriptive accuracy is high. Yet as a hypothesis it is subject to continuous testing. The student should be alert to relate his observations of processes employed in particular scientific investigations to the generalization of the method of science that is Dewey's theory of inquiry.

Comparison of Other Theories of Knowledge with the Scientific Method

The Dewey approach to knowledge, or the knowns, is behavioral as contrasted with mentalistic. The latter, which places a third entity, the mind, between the knower and the knowns has had a long historical development, and is represented by such diverse "isms" as absolute idealism, rationalism, traditional empiricism, and Kantianism. The several explanations of how we know, or the conditions of knowledge, have been called "epistemologies." Theories of knowledge must make connections with "reality," or the structure of the universe, and patterns of explanation of the real world have been called "cosmologies." There has been less agreement about the meaning of "logic." Aristotle's logic was, according to Dewey, a well-structured exposition of the science, or "cosmology," of that early Greek time. Dewey undertook, in his own *Logic*, to exposit the general method employed to establish modern scientific propositions. Some other writers regard logic less functionally, and see in the structure of language some independent conditions for the assertibility of propositions.

Our concern with various viewpoints on ways of knowing or the conditions for knowledge is with a fuller understanding of the positions of modern writers on accounting. Before beginning an examination of some current writings in accounting knowledge, it should be helpful to relate some aspects of those philosophies of knowledge that seem to have had an influence continuing to the present time to the method of modern science.

The problematic situation

The start of inquiry is a "troubled situation." Russell (*An Inquiry Into Meaning and Truth*, p. 407) interprets Dewey's "doubtful situation" in terms of interpersonal doubt, or the doubt which a "trained observer" in the field would have. Thayer (*The Logic of Pragmatism*, p. 72) believes that Dewey's formulation can be modified without damage to the theory, by defining "an indeterminate situation" in terms of observable factors that can be determined to be present or absent by undertaking empirical operations. Dewey himself reiterates the point that the problems that concern him are not personal problems such that their resolution will be identified with the experiencing of personal satisfactions. A problematic situation in accounting involves the use of accounting-treatment rules for corporate financial reporting, and encompasses attitudes of investors and government representatives.

Inquiry for Dewey is behavioral rather than mentalistic. The term "problematic" as modifying "situation" refers to those events that turn the course of behavior from a relative equilibrium state. Inquiry is an adjustive sort of behavior, in which ends in view are associated with correspondingly selected means. (See, for example, a letter written by Dewey, and constituting the Appendix to Dewey and Bentley, *Knowing and the Known*.)

Inquiry as a form of behavior is a component of the environment of concurrent and sequential processes. Its processes have time and space reference. It is not referable to a nonspatial "mind." Dewey and Bentley (*Knowing and the Known*) have elected to use the name "cosmos" for this broadest of concepts for the field in which inquiry and other processes occur.

Dewey insists on time-space descriptions for possible or actual events, but expressly rejects a constraint that space-time be describable in the terms used to express mechanical operations within a system of Cartesian coordinates. He leaves the way open for the development, through experience, of other modes of space-time reference. His insistence is on descriptions in such terms that verifiability through controlled experimentation is a possibility. On the negative side, then, Dewey is fundamentally opposed to metaphysical explanations. Emphasis is on referability to publicly verifiable experience.

Rejection of metaphysical doctrines in explanations of events includes the discard of the notion of a "mind" intermediate between a behaving organism and the environment. Dewey refers to the mentalistic notion of a knowing mind antecedent to knowledge as a doctrine of "self-action." He has fostered the term "transaction" to permit inquiry to continue into all aspects of events. The activity of knowing and the object product of inquiry are dual aspects of inquiry. Borrowing accounting terms, an object which is the conclusion or termination of inquiry might be termed "the debit aspect," and the operations which eventuated in the conclusion of the inquiry or the object might be termed "the credit aspect." The abstract notion of "transaction" is, of course, familiar to accountants. In order to recognize partial stages of inquiry, Dewey accepts the use of the term "interaction" without prejudice to the progression of inquiry to other aspects of transactions. Accounting training has not generally promoted the conception that events or transactions can have more than two relevant aspects.

Naive or natural realism as a philosophical doctrine is a position about the character of an external world, external to a posited "mind." It is represented as an assertion that things are what they seem, or that the mind perceives external objects directly. Among the criticisms of naive realism is the position that the mind can know only "appearances" or perceives only "sense-data." (See, for example, an early statement of the problem by Russell in *The Problems of Philosophy*, pp. 10,11; Russell later introduced the notion of "sensibilia" as "the appearances that things present in places where there are no minds to perceive them," as stated in *My Philosophical Development*, p.105.)

Regardless of a distinction between a "real object" and a sense-datum, assertions are often made in the form that things are "given" to experience. Currently there is evident, as one type of research, the collection and arrangement of data. A companion emphasis is on alternative classifications for the "facts" collected as a means for their interpretation. Accounting has been characterized by the Accounting Terminology Committee of the American Institute of Accountants as a process that emphasizes collection and classification of data [Accounting Research Bulletin No. 9 (Special)]. The current project of the Accounting Principles Board for inventorying and codifying accounting principles has a similar emphasis.

It is a major element in Dewey's hypothesis about the process of inquiry that what can be regarded as "given" to experience is an entire "qualitative situation." Inquiry begins by discriminating certain aspects of that situation, and the selection-rejection can proceed only under the directive capacities of some conception about the efficacy of data for the attainment of the postulated different qualitative situation. Dewey's term for the latter is "end-in-view." Data are selected on the basis of their relevance as means toward the attainment of the end in view. But the context is *not* personal and utilitarian; rather, it is interpersonal and is concerned with conditions that must be satisfied in order for something to be known or warrantedly assertible.

That ideas or conceptions are matters of experience is recognized by Dewey; he is concerned with discriminations among ideas on the basis of their means-characteristics in promoting the attainment of ends in view. It is his position that problem solutions can be attained more effectively by careful distinctions, within inquiry, between "conceptual materials" (ideas, concepts) and existential materials. But an idea can be just as much a tool as can a lever. An integrated set of ideas or conceptions specifying modes of operation and consequences is a hypothesis. The specifications constituting the hypothesis are regarded as possibilities, and the hypothesis is subject to partial verification or disproof through controlled operations with and upon existential materials according to the directives and implications of the hypothesis. Thus, a set of ideas constituting a hypothesis can be quite involved and contain many members. In the process of theory formulation, particular propositions may be referred to a broader set which constitutes a "theory" of the case.

It seems evident that the possibilities for controlled experimentation are smaller in the social sciences than in some of the physical sciences. An associated phenomenon is the persistence of alternative sets of ideas to which reference is made for the explanation of events. Various explanations have been advanced for the rise of modern capitalism, as indicated by Yamey. Many students of accounting currently favor a set of ideas which has been authoritatively represented as "underlying" the use of "utilization" measurements of assets in terms of acquisition-price-aggregate, or "cost." Critics of that "theory," and proponents of the use of economic values in some sense refer their propositions to some portions of an intricate set of ideas in the family of "economic theory." The great need is for experimental testing of the consequences implied by each theory. Ryle (*Dilemmas,* p. 124) has pointed out that dilemmas are experienced when "teams of ideas" conflict.

Identification of the problem

It is Dewey's position that identification of a problem involves selection of data *from* a qualitative situation, toward an end in view. In reference to accounting, the "collection" of data requires the employment of criteria of selection and rejection. The process of problem-identification is progressive. It requires refinements of controlling conceptions according to which selection is made, as well as changes in the included (and excluded) items as a hypothesis is developed. The purpose of the present section of this syllabus is primarily to present expositions of doctrines of "rationalism" and "empiricism" for comparison with the Dewey thesis. The "mediation" aspect of the process of inquiry, involving specialized symbolization and other modes of discourse, will be presented in the following section, where a deductive phase of inquiry will be identified.

It should be emphasized that data are selected *as* facts, guided by conceptions (or ideas) of their means-consequence characteristics in reference to the end in view. Objects are not "given" to experience. Things are objects in view of successful prior inquiry, and are accepted tentatively, where relevant, as appropriate subject-matter for the present inquiry. Both existential data and ideas (conceptions) are operative in the activity of problem-identification. Dewey's term for this joint aspect is "conjugate." The process of selecting some things to serve as facts for the inquiry and of rejecting other possibilities is termed, by Dewey, "affirmation-negation."

Dewey's basic explanation of "idea" is naturalistic and organismic. When the straightforward pattern of activity of an organism (or adjustment to equilibrium) is interrupted, the organism will cast about for means of reestablishing equilibrium (which is accepted as a basic physiological or psychological need). The process of organizing experience in the effort to satisfy the organism's needs involves the consideration of modes of action as possibilities. These possibilities are experienced by the organism as ideas. With advances in civilization, idea development has been explored as an independent undertaking, supported by the use of symbols. The extreme development of symbolization activity is mathematics.

Seventeenth- and eighteenth-century philosophers tended to fix upon one or the other of the "conjugate materials" of inquiry, and to interpret these materials variously as to source and as to the mode of their apprehension by a supposed separate human agent. The "isms" represented here are "rationalism" and "empiricism." The historical progression featured rationalism first.

RATIONALISM.   The aspect of the doctrine of rationalism which is emphasized here is the postulation of a "faculty" of reason that operates to produce concepts. In some manner that faculty is thought to apprehend bits and pieces of "knowledge," or "basic" ideas, and the faculty is able to discriminate true conceptions from fantasy. The essential epistemological feature of rationalism according to Weinberg (*An Examination of Logical Positivism,* p. 188) is "that ratiocination is somehow capable of discovering the truth about the world."

Under one variant of the doctrine of rationalism, ideas are produced independently of "sense-perceptions," although later versions of rationalism did admit the fact of experienced sensations. The name of Descartes is often associated with the notion of rationalism. That noted mathematician-philosopher, in an autobiographical essay called *Discourse on Method*, described a method of progressive doubt which he experienced. Finally Descartes reached a "foundation" in his quest for certainty. He thought he had come upon bedrock when he fastened upon the expression "I think, therefore I am." This was an expression of necessary implication; the process of thinking implied "existence."

The "foundation" seems to have had largely psychological consequences; its recognition by Descartes supported his drive toward mathematical elaboration. The so-called "basic" statement, "Cogito, ergo sum," does not provide a logical basis for Descartes' doctrine of rationalism. It is not a compact premise that contains the secrets of the world, subject only to deductive elaboration. The fundamental assumption that underlay Descartes' claim to have fixed the source of knowledge was the doctrine of a clear and distinct conception coupled with a faith that a series of such clear and distinct conceptions represented the "truth" of the universe. Thus the separation of "illusion" from "truth" was made to depend on personal standards.

What is the current significance of a doctrine of rationalism? The ultimate appeal to a personal process of attaining to the "truth" tended to support authoritarian institutions. Social movements that emphasized personal liberty would not find the doctrine of rationalism attractive or suitable, and in fact a competing doctrine of "empiricism" developed in England. Interconnections between rationalism and authoritarianism are evident today. Modern accounting writers seem, in some instances, to base their recommendations for accounting-treatment rules on notions of self-evident or clearly conceived concepts which, when entering "into system," provide a sufficient criterion of the "truth" of those and deductively derived propositions. Concepts are viewed as ends in themselves rather than as instruments for ordering existential data whose interactions determine the content of knowledge.

Where the test of clarity and distinctness of discrete conceptions is subordinated to aesthetic perceptions of ideas-in-system, an additional metaphysical (not verifiable by those tests which by interpersonal agreement are experiences) factor is introduced. For example, Joachim (*The Nature of Truth*) follows the Hegelian notion of an ideal of "whole and complete truth," and supports the coherence theory of truth as providing apprehension of the "closest approximation" to the unknowable whole. In the contemporary field of accounting writers, Littleton seems to be the closest proponent of the coherence point of view for establishing the verity of accounting doctrines. This characteristic of Littleton's writing will be more fully examined in a section of the following chapter.

It must be recognized that scientific theories also constitute systems of interrelated ideas. But the latter are selected, not for their "inherent" coherence value, but as approximate descriptions of experientially supported events.

A current problem in the interpretation of accounting writings is the circumstance that the writers frequently rest particular statements on a supporting framework of interrelated ideas without sufficiently specifying that framework. Ryle (*Dilemmas*, p. 16) refers to "traffic-blocks" which occur when words that have a particular function in one reference system are used to do work in some other system of ideas. Does the word "accrue" have a single, definite meaning for accounting? It has been found useful in accounting for events such as rent or interest obligations and payments. Can an inquiry leading to a position on income tax allocation be guided by an assertion that income taxes "accrue"?

Ryle (*Dilemmas*, p. 85) also decries the use of "smother-expressions," whose ambiguities deny access to those distinctions that are necessary for knowing the intended function of the word in a particular system of ideas. In the assertion that inventories should be priced at current cost, is the emphasis on "cost" or on "current"? The latter interpretation opens up an extensive field of "price theory" in economic analysis, yet its acceptance for committing action may be tied to habitual attitudes toward "cost" pricing. Or, as another problem, how does accelerated depreciation based on historical cost perform functions attributable to replacement-"cost" depreciation?

The rather generally shared feeling that knowledge should be restricted to events which have a basis in "experience" has had several interpretations. Among these are a traditional theory of "empiricism" as associated with John Locke and other English writers, and a more modern "empiricism" reflected in the writings of Russell and ascribed also to A. J. Ayer. Each of these will be very briefly described to serve as a basis for comparison with the Dewey exposition of the method of modern science.

EMPIRICISM: THE TRADITIONAL VIEW. Traditional empiricism as it developed in England in reaction to continental rationalism had both negative and positive aspects of importance. On the negative side, there was a denial of any faculty of reason which could apprehend truths, and which could discriminate true from false concepts on the basis of their clarity of apperception. The explanation of Locke, with whom this early English empiricism is often associated, did utilize a person's "mind," but with a function different from that of the rationalist explanation. In the empiricists' view, Man possessed a mind which passively received, ordered, and combined "sense-impressions." The source of sense-impressions was, according to Locke, the external world.

Berkeley, too, accepted sense-impressions as the basic element of experience. He did not doubt that Johnson felt pain when he kicked a stone. The peculiarity of Berkeley's position was his ascription of sensations (or "ideas") to Mind as an original source. Locke and Berkeley agreed that what one knew was what was "inside his head."

Locke assumed the existence of an external world as in fact the source of sense-impressions. Since the subject-matter of experience was sense-impressions, which were mental phenomena, the question of the character of the external world was posed. We noted Berkeley's rejection of the notion that there was an external world, or any material other than spirit. Locke argued that the sense impressions were copies of external-world objects, and that these were supplemented by a few other ideas such as the idea of God, apprehended intuitively according to the rationalist mode.

It has been said that Locke would have felt at home with modern science, as evidenced by the character of his distinction between "primary" and "secondary" qualities. The former had a source in external-world objects; secondary qualities had their source in characteristics of the mind. The so-called primary qualities included extension (for example, length), and were the kinds of aspect with which physical sciences have been concerned. Examples of the secondary class of qualities are color and taste. The assumed "substance" which "carried" the primary qualities was an enigma to Locke, who could describe it only as "I know not what."

A sign relation rather than a copy relation seems closer to the modern scientific viewpoint. Under a modification of the Lockian view, sense-impressions were regarded as signs or indicators of real-world objects or events which permitted manipulation of, or personal adaptation to, the external world. The signification function of ideas was also a part of Berkeley's explanation; however, what a sense-impression signified for Berkeley was another *idea*, leading ultimately to Divine Mind.

The implication of sensationalistic empiricism for denial of knowledge of an external world was carried out in detail by David Hume. And it was Hume's "general outlook" that Bertrand Russell adopted for the development of *An Inquiry into Meaning and Truth*.

EMPIRICISM: A MODERN VIEW. In Russell's view (*An Inquiry into Meaning and Truth*) the truth of any statement was to be ascertained by first reducing the statement to its component basic sentences, and then relating the basic sentences to certain individually experienced events, not further reducible, which provide whatever warrant there is for asserting the truth or falsity of the basic sentences. The terms "factual premises" and "sense-data" have been used to refer to such ultimate experiences. Russell makes "noticing" an element in this interpretation of experience, as a refinement of the "sense-datum" position. G. E. Moore has figured prominently in the elaboration and illustration of the concept of "sense data." A. J. Ayer (*The Problem of Knowledge,* p. 152) seems to reject Russell's reducibility argument, and views percepts more functionally as constituting the experiences that "count in favor" of the truth of those statements which refer to "physical objects."

Another kind of reductionism, with which Carnap's name has been associated, attempts to reduce statements (languages) to forms to which syntactical models can be applied with a result of determining the truth or falsity of the statements. An extreme position considers that the basic or model language contains its own "objective criteria" for determining the truth or falsity of the included sentences. This is an intricate area for professional philosophers and is mentioned here only because of a modern tendency in accounting writings to use references to such things as "the tremendous power of mathematics," or "modern developments in communications theory," or "the rules of syntax" in emotive ways. Russell has stated that his emphasis on linguistics has been lessened, but that he is still psychologically tied to a belief that "the structure of the world" may be revealed partly by "the study of syntax" (*An Inquiry into Meaning and Truth*, pp. 5 and 438).

Russell has charged that Dewey did not sufficiently explain the relation of scientific propositions to the kinds of nonverbal events or percepts which Russell regarded as ultimates, and in general that Dewey did not sufficiently specify what he meant by "experience." What Dewey did consider as "given" in experience was an undiscriminated qualitative situation, and not "sense-data." Problem identification requires discriminations within the field. Certain data are selected and ordered in accordance with controlling conceptions about the manner in which the data may be related as means to the attainment of an end in view. Russell's notion of percept has a character of finality. Each ultimate experience is taken by him to add something to the total knowledge. For Dewey, discriminated data are selected tentatively, and their provisional character as knowledge is further tested by the consequences flowing from their employment in the later inquiry. Apparently, experience is a matter of interpersonal agreement for Dewey. In what sense is the term "experience" used in certain accounting justifications of particular treatment rules? What are the elements of experience in the criterion "experienced judgment"?

Still another form of reductionism is the association of scientific generalizations to "familiar correlations" which are accepted as the most basic matters of experience (Bridgman, *The Logic of Modern Physics*, p. 27). "Experience" here seems to be a matter of professional agreement about the interpersonal phenomena that are to be regarded as basic, and is itself presumably testable by the consequences of subsequent operations which were motivated by the prior experience. The latter view seems to accord with Dewey's stated position.

In a later section of this syllabus it will be noted that the method of science is circular and self-correcting. The testing may establish consistency of the results of the experiment with the set of conceptions that initially controlled the discriminative selection of things to serve as data. The possibility that the entire hypothesis structure may sometime need to be discarded for a range of inquiry has been vividly illustrated on occasion in the physical sciences, notably in the construct of space-time.

Identification of a problem and refinement of hypotheses differ in degree only. And refinement of a hypothesis may efficiently utilize intermediate means for indicating possibilities with manifold implications. In the latter process discourse, including mathematical formulation, enters as a prominent operation.

Knowledge is not immediate

Dewey pointed out that both rationalism and empiricism focused, respectively, on one but not both of the two types of materials involved in inquiry, those which Dewey calls "ideational" and "existential." And the approach of traditional empiricism was psychological under an outmoded psychology.

Dewey's approach was a rejection both of metaphysics and of the psychological bias of empiricism. It also rejected the mentalism implicit in setting up a human mind as intermediary between the world of events and knowings.

Yet Dewey gave explicit recognition to the functional role of mediating elements in the process of inquiry. Hypotheses may extensively develop possibilities of interconnections between means and consequences. As a possibility, a hypothesis is an ordering of meanings, or data at the conceptual level. In refining interconnections among meanings, discourse has been found efficient. Meanings may be more readily handled through symbols, and the extensive symbolization systems of mathematics may be employed in correspondence with possibilities of interactions among the existential data under the guidance of the directive hypothesis. It is in this stage of inquiry that deduction as a special phase of the inquiry process may be identified in particular instances.

Chambers, Devine, and Mattessich are among accounting writers who have emphasized deductive systems (or interpreted mathematical systems). In their zeal accounting writers have sometimes suggested that the scientific method is identified with the adoption of axioms and rules of operation, and the working out of the implied set of relationships among the meanings so determined. Dewey has pointed to a broader scope of scientific method, and has recognized deduction as part of a more extensive and intricate process. Possibly the standard textbook illustration of deduction is the categorical syllogism, where the "conclusion" is determined by a drawing-out of the meanings implicit in the logical premises. Implications of scientific hypotheses, however, seem seldom to be presented in as simple an arrangement as in the traditional categorical syllogism.

Some types of "logically necessary" relationships were studied many years ago. For instance, Aristotle was interested in the relationship between "all" and "some" (for example, in *The Posterior Analytics,* Book I, Chapter 21). In more recent years attempts have been made to symbolize relationships among word meanings extensively, and to formulate implications among the word meanings. Among the names prominently associated with developments in symbolic logic are George Boole, Bertrand Russell, and Arthur E. Whitehead. A contrast is often made in philosophically inclined writings between "necessary" (or deductively implicated) relationships and "contingent" relations, where the latter are to be determined empirically or factually. What is sometimes insufficiently emphasized is that any relationship of meanings constituting a hypothesis is a "necessary" relationship if it constitutes a directive for the performance of existential operations that will provide new data serving to test the hypothesis. Certain rules have been developed, as generalizations of procedures in inquiry, for testing the consistency of statements that make up hypotheses. The latter are sometimes referred to as rules of "necessary" implication, illustrated by the requirement that *all* of a kind includes a *part* of the same kind or class.

Dewey puts great stress upon the functional status of relationships among meanings. Forms of logic (recognized types of implications) are explained by him as having developed in the process of inquiry. The logical forms have "accrued." Their continued acceptance is a consequence of their successful employment in the process by which warranted assertions are obtained. Their explanation is not metaphysical; rules of syntax do not provide an external standard for judging the warrantability of assertions; and "logic" cannot be expected to provide an antecedent "foundation" for mathematics. A practical corollary is that every writer should be expected to declare fully the sense in which he uses the terms "logic" and "logical."

In the preceding paragraphs "rationalism" and "empiricism" were each related to Dewey's exposition of the process of inquiry as illustrating the persuasiveness of doctrines that touch on, although they do not completely represent, processes by which warranted assertions are reached. Kant (*Critique of Pure Reason*) attempted to combine continental rationalism and English empiricism into a unique system for which the term "Kantianism" is appropriate. The latter system had considerable influence among German scientists and German philosophers particularly, and this mode of thought was specifically recognized as an obstacle to acceptance of the logical empiricism propounded by the so-called Vienna Circle from just before the beginning of World War I to just before the beginning of World War II (Frank, *Modern Science and Its Philosophy*).

For Kant, the mind contributed two important classes of "forms." The forms of space and time "exist in the mind a priori" and exclusively. That is, space and time are not relations of external world objects. These forms are also preconditions for the understanding of the world. The actual process of understanding entails the impressment of a priori "categories," or forms of understanding such as causation or substance which are characteristic of the mind, upon the "noumena" which are assumed to constitute the external world. The consequent "phenomena" or appearances are thus products of both mind and experiences. Noumena, or the underlying data of experience, have meaning only because "the understanding thinks the connection of things a priori."

Dewey has reiterated the importance of reference to operations to be employed with and upon specified materials under stated conditions in order to reach postulated consequences. This emphasis on operations, and upon operational meanings of concepts has been shared with Bridgman (*The Logic of Modern Physics*), James (*Pragmatism*), and Peirce, whose pioneer thinking Dewey and others widened. Such an approach is in sharp contrast with the anchoring of statements upon "first principles," or upon concepts or doctrines accepted intuitively, or asserted "a priori," or on other grounds independently of their function in, and testing by, inquiry.

A related idea in the context of mediation is that mathematical systems have reference to existential possibilities when used in inquiry. A mathematics-trained person may prefer to develop mathematical systems (or systems of logical calculus) with great freedom and to emphasize the "problem" of selecting that system which seems best to match the circumstances of the "corresponding" real-world "problem." Superimposing a number of branding irons on the steer's hide will indicate the ranch to which the previously branded steer belongs.

It appears that accounting developments to date have been largely heuristic, in the sense that "enlightened guesses" have been expanded into precepts which are utilized for guiding actions. The precepts may represent "expert" trial-and-error methods, where "experience" in the area suggests lines of relationship. The various guiding rules are largely independent rather than being highly generalized into common system. Applications of mathematics to some business situations in the spirit of "operations research" may also be characterized as heuristic. Hypotheses that were developed from "suggested" mathematical models can provide directives for the ordering of operations upon specified materials. Study of the consequences can help to develop "explanations" of business processes through the insight into interactions gained from observation of the controlled operations which were directed by the mathematical model.

Experimentalism and the self-corrective characteristic of the scientific method

While controlled experimentation has been the cornerstone of the scientific method, the testability of hypotheses by reference to observation of consequences for their agreement with the results postulated by the hypothesis is a matter of degree. It is generally held that experimentation is not as prominent a feature of operations of inquiry in the social sciences as it is in a number of the physical sciences. Limitations on experimentation for testing the theory that modern capitalism depended on double-entry bookkeeping for its expansion were noted in Chapter 1 of this syllabus. But the function of experimentation in developing the warranted assertibility of propositions is no less important in the one area than in the other.

The tentativeness of scientific conclusions even under favorable conditions for experimentation is an aspect of the interpretation of the scientific method as self-correcting. Objects are identified with terminations of inquiries. Fire is an object or class of objects by reason of certain consequences of operations. It is not necessary for the status of an object that it be touchable or kickable. A rainbow can be an object constituting the termination of inquiry. Process is a key idea, and processes occur at different rates. A marble statue has a low process rate compared with fog.

Objects that are the terminations of prior inquiry become the subject matter of later inquiry. Heat-resistant metal alloys become incorporated in unmanned re-entry capsules. The consequences that ensue when objects are employed as subject-matters on the basis of expectations about interactions have an important bearing on the warrantability of prior conclusions about the subject matters. Other metal-alloy possibilities may need to be explored. And objects that are the terminations of current inquiries must meet subsequent tests of consequences, as a condition for continuance of warranted assertibility of the proposition that represents the conclusion as a particular object in terms of interactions with other objects. The circularity of the scientific method is factual; this characteristic has accrued in the process of the relatively successful employment of that method in inquiry.

Analogous to the back-and-forth movement between objects of prior inquiry and subject-matters of present inquiry, suggested in processes involving the suitability of metal alloys for re-entry capsules, is the interplay of existential and conceptual materials in present inquiry. Facts are not given to inquiry; data are selected from a field in accordance with their postulated means-characteristics in relation to ends in view. The refinement of a hypothesis can involve a new selection and ordering of existential materials, and observations of interactions among selected materials may require a reshaping of the hypothesis which again requires a different set of data. At various points the hypothesis may be tested by using one or more deductive corollaries of the hypothesis as directives for the modification of the environment and observing the consequence in correspondence with the consequences postulated by the hypothesis.

For example, the determination of sequences, which constitute an explanation of the malaria disease historically, involved suggestions for a hypothesis from observation of instances of parasitic diseases. But a bacillic source of malaria was also not inconsistent with observations on characteristics of the malaria patient. Testing of the parasite theory required the institution of new operations and the development of new data in correspondence with the conception constituting the parasite theory. If the disease were of parasitic origin, then correspondences should be observable between the life cycle of the suspected parasite and sequential phases of the condition of the patient. Data developed in these directions tended to confirm the parasite hypothesis. Other operations were also suggested and conducted, as in the controlled biting of certain warm-blooded animals by selected strains of mosquitoes. The interplay of existential operations on the basis of differential traits of objects, and hypotheses setting out modes of interaction as possibilities is an important aspect of the method of science.

It is an important part of Dewey's theory that there is no separable operation that constitutes "induction" in the sense in which that term has traditionally been used. Keynes (*Scope and Method of Political Economy*) refers to "purely inductive methods" (p. 178) and to "inductive determinations of premises" and "inductive verification of conclusions" (p. 227). John Stuart Mill (*A System of Logic*) contrasts "induction" and "ratiocination" (p. 125) and significantly refers to "the Baconian conception of Induction" (p. 227). Under the Baconian scheme, the critical operation for inquiry is "observation." The observation of a "sufficient number" of events is supposed to permit the mind to isolate one or more common elements, and to formulate a generalization whose validity depends only on the "accuracy" of the observations and generalization.

Current literature, including accounting writing, often sets off "induction" as an independent mode of acquiring knowledge, usually opposed to "deduction." Or the supposedly independent "methods" will be associated as, in some undisclosed manner, cooperating in providing knowledge. It is because many arguments are hinged on a meaning of "induction" which is not represented in Dewey's exposition of the scientific method that it is important for the student to read the treatment of the term "induction" in the Dewey reading assignments.

It is possible that some accounting writers use the term "induction" in a more sophisticated sense than is represented in, say, John Stuart Mill's *A System of Logic*. Bertrand Russell contends that we learn something from each individual experience in the sense of apprehension through percepts. And it may be that a progressive simplification of experiences will eventuate into a recognition of the structure of the universe and a complete understanding of its processes. Some writers refer to inductive processes as psychological rather than logical. The direction of research effort, then, would be toward the bases for discriminating those features of experience which "count as evidence" for assertions about basic events.

If induction is correctly characterized as a psychological problem, the fact that persons have expectations on the basis of their experiences is not explicable within what Weinberg interprets as the Logical Positivist principles (*An Examination of Logical Positivism*). As with most "isms," there are variations in the characterization of "logical positivism." The early developments in a school of logical positivism (or logical "empiricism") are interestingly told by Philipp Frank, a member of the Vienna Circle (*Modern Science and Its Philosophy*). More recently Bertrand Russell stated that he attached less importance to the study of linguistics, and more importance to the connection of experiences with basic sentences, than do certain other members of the logical positivist persuasion (*An Inquiry Into Meaning and Truth*, pp. 5, 6). The influence of Rudolf Carnap in the logical positivist school is widely recognized, and is recognized by Morton White's inclusion of an excerpt from Carnap's writings in the former's book on *The Age of Analysis* (pp. 203-225, with a descriptive foreword). The relation of the logical positivist position to "induction" is suggested in Carnap, *The Nature and Application of Inductive Logic.*

Warranted assertibility and "truth"

Dewey has tried to describe the conditions that must be satisfied if an assertion is to have a warranted status according to the method of modern science. Those conditions have been found through experience and have been tested by experience. They are subject to modification by future experience. The focus is on correspondence of change, and the criterion of assertibility is the correspondence of actual with postulated consequences. These features may have prompted Thayer to call Dewey's hypothesis a "co-respondence" theory (*The Logic of Pragmatism*).

Dewey's emphasis on warranted assertibility has been interpreted as a denial that the term "true" is applicable to any proposition other than to that conclusion or object which is the termination of inquiry. Prior to the termination of an inquiry, propositions are either efficient or inefficient in promoting a solution of the problem.

Bertrand Russell has suggested that Dewey chose to bypass the term "truth" because of its connotation of finality, and that at any one time Dewey does recognize a division of propositions between those that are and are not warrantedly assertible (between "sheep" and "goats" as stated by Russell in *An Inquiry into Meaning and Truth*, pp. 409, 410). However, Dewey's relative disuse of the term "true" can be explained also by his emphasis on existential processes as providing the warrant for propositions, as contrasted with the emphasis placed by certain other writers on words and sentences, and on an interpretation of meanings by reference to Russell's "factual premisses" or to "the objective criteria provided by a syntactical system." Russell characterized his own views as representing a correspondence theory of truth (*An Inquiry into Meaning and Truth*, p. 363). The correspondence upon which Russell relied was basically between sentences in general and those sentences that describe experiences, and between the latter and the irreducible or ultimate nonverbal events that are the source of meanings.

The traditional coherence view of truth is not a part of the Dewey formulation. The coherence theory of truth as it was described by Joachim (*The Nature of Truth*) was also rejected by Russell. The coherence criterion has already been noted in this syllabus. It may be that Littleton's *The Structure of Accounting Theory* is ultimately reducible to this doctrine. Coherence in the Joachim (and Hegelian) view has a reference to an unknown and unknowable "whole," to which a system of ideas is related as a part. However, coherence may be loosely interpreted as (internal) consistency, and the latter is a necessary or implicatory relationship among meanings in a system of ideas, including a scientific hypothesis.

Dewey on the classical Greek influence

Dewey is not alone in trying to relate logic functionally to operations in science. J. S. Mill represented his "system of logic" as "a connected view of the principles of evidence and the methods of scientific investigation." According to Dewey, Mill retained earlier psychological misconceptions and erroneously represented the method of modern science. Aristotle's logic (the *Organon*), on the other hand, is said to be an adequate functional account of the relation of meanings to the science of his time. The major difference, then, between the logic of Aristotle and the logic of Dewey is in the character and content of the respective sciences. The importance of Aristotle's *Logic* today is in the modern penchant for using the classical language, constructed for its reference to a Greek cosmology, in the context of modern scientific inquiry.

It is not difficult to find accounting writings that base statements upon an assumed force of ideas represented by words such as "essence," "nature," "substance," or "ideal." Some reference to Aristotelian logic is necessary for an understanding of an important segment of modern accounting literature. Dewey has repeatedly analyzed Aristotle's logic, and he devoted an entire chapter (Chapter 5, pp. 81-98) to it and its implications in his *Logic, The Theory of Inquiry.*

Joseph Ratner, in an "Introduction to John Dewey's Philosophy" (*Intelligence in the Modern World*), emphasized two aspects of Dewey's interpretation of Greek science and logic, the "spectator theory" and the "quest for certainty." The latter phrase was also the title of an important essay by Dewey. The "spectator theory" referred to an asserted Greek viewpoint of the "mind" as passively observing happenings and, under appropriate circumstances, apprehending truths of Nature. The "quest for certainty" includes a reference to the Greek notion of a world of fixed substances, each unique, and together constituting the whole of the universe. Knowledge of the "essences" that composed the universe was obtained by specially favored or philosophical minds by a process of eduction through contemplative observation of (changing) phenomena. The ideal was contrasted with the material, and the universal with the accidental.

The main burden of logic as an explanation of the Greek cosmology was to define and to classify. It was by definition that the essence or unique universal substance was represented, and it was by classification that the manifestation of the hierarchy of fixed substances in observable events was to be recognized. A definition was constituted by the genus, or characterization of the unique essence, and by differentia, or indications of relations within the hierarchy of fixed substances. The demonstrative syllogism was the mode of extending knowledge, through pointing out the connections that inhered in the "necessary basic truths" represented by the premises of the syllogism. It was categorical in a functional, and not a merely formal, sense.

The relation of the particular "theories" exposited by Paton and Littleton or implied in Accounting Research Studies No. 1 and No. 3 to the method of science will be explored in Chapters 6 through 9 of this syllabus. It is the purpose of Chapter 5 to examine the accounting literature for relatively prominent instances of the reference of accounting theorization to the scientific method and to note the requirements set out by accounting writers as conditions for an accounting theory. Most of the questions on this phase of the course have been deferred to Chapter 5, where the accounting writings assigned for study are brought into connection with the thread of the scientific method developed in Chapter 4.

READINGS

DEWEY, JOHN, *Logic, The Theory of Inquiry*, Chapters 1 and 21.
NAGEL, ERNEST, "The Value-Oriented Bias of Social Inquiry," in *The Structure of Science*, pp. 485-502.

QUESTIONS

1. Salter (*A Critical Review of Research in Land Economics*) sees science presented, in a 1928 Handbook on Research Method and Procedure in Agricultural Economics, as a process of "collection, summarizing, analysis, judgment, and presentation of numerical data of mass phenomena." What similarities and differences do you see with the definition of *accounting* advanced by the Committee on Terminology of the American Institute of Accountants? In your opinion does the quoted statement correctly represent the core of the scientific method?

2. Can an end in view, as a possible resolution of an unsettled situation toward which particular data are selected as means, be

reasonably termed a "postulate"? A "postulated outcome"? May a problem-solving approach in inquiry be termed a "postulational" approach? May "postulates" be identified as the conditions that must be met if the indicated consequence is to be realized?

3. Is the contention that the scientific method is not applicable to social sciences a warranted conclusion based on experimental testing? Is it a deductive conclusion derived from an assumption that the method of science is characterized by a purpose to find invariable relations among experienced data? Is the assumption a correct one?

4. If the method of science is characterized by inquiry directed toward problem solving in the sense of unification of unsettled situations, what is the meaning of "an ideal solution" in this context? Is the latter identified by dream or wish qualities as distinguished from a pattern of means-consequences? Is the measurement of change in value of enterprise resources an ideal solution to some current accounting problems? Are there imperatives that compel action toward unattainable ideals?

5. What two descriptions of "value judgment" are presented in the assigned reading in Nagel, *The Structure of Science?* What sense or senses of the term is (are) used in the following quotation from Mautz ("Accounting As a Social Science," *The Accounting Review*, April 1963, p. 323) regarding a choice between FIFO and LIFO inventory methods: "Selection of one of these methods over the other is a value judgment and if accounting is ever to earn social science status it must provide bases for such decisions"?

5

Conditions
for Accounting Theory According
to Contemporary Accounting Writings

Most of the literature on specific criteria for evaluating accounting
theory has appeared since 1950. An earlier classic is J. B. Canning's
The Economics of Accountancy, in which accounting methodology
was evaluated by reference to standards of statistical validity. Writings of DR Scott over a long period of years advocated greater utilization of statistical inference in accountants' judgments. Many
isolated (noncumulative) instances may be found of lip service accorded the "scientific method." Some writers ask whether accounting *is* a science. The latter question is now tending to yield to the
more fruitful question, "In what manner is the scientific method
applicable to the materials of accounting?"

In a 1953 publication, *Structure of Accounting Theory,* A. C.
Littleton attempted to relate practices of accountants to a generalized statement of theory. The need to place accounting propositions in a thought structure broader than "evolution" or "agreement"
had been recognized as early as 1940, in the publication of the
Paton and Littleton monograph, *An Introduction to Corporate Accounting Standards.* The significance of the *Structure* publication
is in its recognition of the need to provide standards for evaluating
particular accounting theory formulations.

Littleton's approach to the conditions for accounting theory
seems, in some sections, to resemble the philosophical approach
labeled "traditional empiricism." The observation of the practice of
accounting is the key to knowledge, and accounting theory is an
ordered structuring of generalizations on practice. On the other
hand, Littleton's notion of a "cause" which directs accounting "evolution" toward some presently unidentified goal, evident in his *Accounting Evolution to 1900,* is expressed also in Littleton's emphasis

on "interrelatedness" and structural "wholeness" as characteristics of "good" theory. A number of the questions that follow these comments indicate a possible foundation, for Littleton's approach, in a coherence theory of truth.

In 1955 R. J. Chambers published an article which he called "Blueprint for a Theory of Accounting." This article included an "exposure list" of four major propositions as postulates, axioms, or building blocks for an accounting theory structure, as illustrative of the process of theory formulation. Attention was drawn more strongly to the "Blueprint" article after Littleton criticized Chambers' premises ("Choice among Alternatives," *The Accounting Review*, July 1956) and Chambers responded to the charges ("Detail for a Blueprint," *The Accounting Review*, April 1957). Late in 1960 Chambers proliferated his thesis in an article called "The Conditions of Research in Accounting" (*Journal of Accountancy*, December 1960). Other relevant writings by Chambers include *Towards a General Theory of Accounting* and *The Resolution of Some Paradoxes in Accounting*.

We shall give particular attention to two additional articles dealing with criteria for accounting theory formulation. These articles constitute a pair. The first is by Carl Devine, "Research Methodology and Accounting Theory Formation" (*The Accounting Review*, July 1960). The second is by Norton Bedford and Nicholas Dopuch, "Research Methodology and Accounting Theory—Another Perspective" (*The Accounting Review*, July 1961). These articles should be studied for the reflection of the authors' views on the appropriateness of the scientific method to the field of the social sciences and to the subject matter of accounting, and for their indicated directions for accounting research. As a collateral undertaking the reader may be interested in considering whether "communications theory" (Bedford and Baladouni, "A Communication Theory Approach to Accounting," *The Accounting Review*, October 1962) represents a new approach for arriving at warranted accounting propositions.

READINGS

LITTLETON, A. C., *Structure of Accounting Theory*, Chapters 8, 10, 11, and 12.

CHAMBERS, R. J., "Blueprint for a Theory of Accounting," *Accounting Research*, 1955, Vol. 6, pp. 17-25.

LITTLETON, A. C., "Choice among Alternatives," *The Accounting Review*, July 1956, pp. 363-370.

CHAMBERS, R. J., "Detail for a Blueprint," *The Accounting Review*, April 1957, pp. 206-215.

DEVINE, C. T., "Research Methodology and Accounting Theory Formation," *The Accounting Review*, July 1960, pp. 387-399.

BEDFORD, N. M., AND NICHOLAS DOPUCH, "Research Methodology and Accounting Theory—Another Perspective," *The Accounting Review*, July 1961, pp. 351-361.

QUESTIONS

GROUP 1.   ON LITTLETON'S STRUCTURE OF ACCOUNTING THEORY

1. One difficulty in interpreting Littleton's *Structure of Accounting Theory* is that his hypostatized concepts need to be reordered and interpreted as propositions so that his meanings about conditions that inquiry must satisfy will be apparent. Can you relate the following statements to Dewey's exposition of the method of science? ". . . the nature of theory is to explain . . ." ". . . theory reasons from purposes outward toward actions . . ."

2. Taking Littleton's use of the term "practice" in the sense of "fact and action" as contrasted with mental operations, how does the notion compare with that of interdependency between data and conceptions used to control their selection and use?

3. Is "practice" in the sense of a generalization about characteristic activities of accountants clearly different from "theory"? Relate Littleton's distinction to the method of science, in which data are ordered in ways designed to test the hypothesis, as evidence that the consequences predicted by the theory do in fact follow.

4. At some points in his Chapter 8, Littleton makes statements which suggest that experimentation is a necessary phase of inquiry. For example, he refers to Darwin's observations of animals and plants in relation to Darwin's theory of the origin of species. How does Littleton's exposition accord with Dewey's statement of the method of science? Does Littleton write as if data were given in experience and the theory phase consisted of organizing repeated observations? How do you interpret Littleton's allusion to the "real significance of the collected facts"?

5. What evidence do you find in Littleton's Chapter 8 and Chapter 10 of the dependence of Littleton's propositions upon conceptions associated with early Greek views on the structure of the world and on Aristotelian logic? How does Littleton's meaning of "definition" compare with that of Aristotle? Is definition a tool for the promotion of inquiry, and therefore adaptable to the directions taken by inquiry? Or is the meaning of definition better expressed as a process of placing a defined thing within a fixed structure of Nature, such that the essential quality or genus of the item is made evident and proper differentiations are made from other and essentially different substances? Which of the two approaches tends to reinforce the rejection of income tax allocation on the ground that the proper definition of liability limits the latter category to a legally enforceable claim?

6. Dewey uses the term "definition" to refer to characters as identifying *meanings,* as abstractions. Dewey distinguishes *classes* of existential things related according to their modes of interactions. Meanings, at the nonexistential or conceptual level, are collected into *categories.* Does "principle" fall in the area of *classes* or *categories?*

7. When Littleton defines a specific accounting principle, does he intend that the meaning is fixed for all purposes? That the principle expresses a part of the order of Nature? Littleton seems to prefer that meaning for "principle" which verbalizes a relation between an objective and a means. In what sense, then, is a "principle" a "tool of theory"?

8. Does Littleton regard alternative formulations of objective-means relations as possibilities for inclusion as components of a "theory," with the choice between the alternative formulations to be made on independent grounds? What criteria come to your mind for choosing among alternative statements of either objective-means or means-consequence relations?

9. A basic proposition in Aristotelian logic is the joinder of a "subject" with an "attribute" or "predicate" through the use of a "copula." For example, in the expression "the apple is red," the attribute "redness" is joined with the subject "apple." Littleton says that a "definition" is a "verbal statement distinguishing several attributes." Is this form of statement consistent with an assumption that "facts" are "given" in experience, and that the problem of "theory" is to grasp their "real significance" or "essential nature"?

10. Littleton says that the "existence" of accounting theory is

"justified by the help it can render to clear thinking in accounting."
What are the specifications of "clear thinking"? You may recall
Descartes' test of a true concept as the clarity with which that concept appeared to the reasoning faculty of the mind. Is "clear thinking" primarily a psychological question? A matter of individual and
personal experience?

11. Littleton views accounting theory as explanations of accounting practices. And he distinguishes classes of "good" and
"bad" practices. If one finds the reason behind "bad" practices,
will the theory be bad even though the explanation of the practice
is well done? Or can a "bad" practice have a "reason"? Is a "bad"
practice distinguished by its incomprehensibility or nonsense, or by
the moral implications of the means-consequences pattern?

12. In his discussion of "truths in accountancy," Littleton uses
degree-terms, such as "carefully," "closely," "clearly," and "strong."
Is the factor of "a strong sense of relevance" a psychological factor
or a metaphysical factor of the order of "intuition"?

13. Littleton suggests that "principles" of accounting may
"emerge" after accounting "truths" are adequately verbalized. Does
he refer to more than a process of identifying deductions that are
implicit in premises? What is the meaning of "emerging"? Is Littleton implying that there is a *first cause* operating, in the sense that
there is a "final destiny" for accounting which has its explanation in
metaphysical doctrines?

14. Littleton says "theory leans strongly toward consistency
among its ideas." Does this statement reflect the acceptance of a
coherence theory of truth? Is there some other ground for accepting statements as "principles even though they do not derive from
controlled experimentation and do not aspire to the status of
laws"?

15. Does the acceptance of Littleton's propositions tend
toward a mode of thought that favors experimentation with accounting techniques; or one that equates existing practices with
"good" practices and identifies "theory" with the rationalization, as
justification, of existing practices? Which type of approach to the
valuation of practice would be critical and which would be doctrinal? Which approach is more compatible with the scientific
method?

16. What is Littleton's statement of the "principle" that tends
to justify the accountants' reliance upon the "historical cost stand-

ard"? (You will recall that a principle, for Littleton, starts with a verbalization of a purpose in association with a means.)

17. What is the basis for accepting Littleton's statement of the conditions under which "transactions" are "rendered homogeneous"? Is the warrantedness of Littleton's assertion that "homogeneity" is an attribute of acquisition price made to depend in any sense on a tracing and evaluation of consequences? Or is the foundation a coherence theory of "truth"? Is the talismanic operation a "chaining into a circle"?

18. In Chapter 10 Littleton makes a statement which may be significant for an interpretation of his conditions for the warrantedness of propositions, or his "tests for principles" whose acceptance will deductively determine other rules of treatment. He quotes approvingly from his article in the March, 1938, *Accounting Review* on "Tests for Principles." He there recognizes three modes of attaining to "truth" in accounting. With a slight modification of the verb forms, it may be said that the processes for establishing accounting truths are, alternatively, "generalization out of practical experience," "deduction from stated premises which are accepted as true in themselves," or "demonstrated to be true by argument." Does Littleton regard induction and deduction as separable operations? Is Littleton saying that there are two (or three) independent ways of attaining knowledge, in contrast with the single methodology called "the scientific method"?

19. Compare Littleton's explanation of the "deductive approach" to knowledge with Dewey's explanation of the deductive phase of inquiry. Do you consider the terms "true" and "known to be true" as too strong, too definite, from the point of view that inquiry is continuous, and that conclusions of inquiry are tentative objects? Is there some value in reserving the term "inference" for the positing of relations among existential propositions, and using, say, the term "implication" for designating the deductive relationships among propositions at the conceptual level?

20. Does Littleton intend, by the phrase "prior propositions known to be true," more than an ordering of propositions according to their meanings-relationships? Or are some "basic" propositions to be established as "true" by rationalistic or other means in some absolute sense? (The *Accounting Research Study No. 1,* to be discussed in Chapter 8 of this syllabus, raises a similar question.)

21. What does Littleton use to support the statement that

"the best practices—those reflecting a principle—will be found to rest on moral grounds"? Is this different from saying that ethical judgments are involved in the selection of means in correspondence with ends in view?

22. Is the use of "values" rather than "costs" in financial statements "logically" dependent on the adoption of an assumption that the enterprise in question will be dissolved? Is "liquidating value" the only alternative "value" to historical cost?

23. Is Littleton's conclusion that the challenges of price changes do not invalidate the several stated "principles" based largely on the way in which his "principles" are stated? Should the emphasis in accounting research be on formulating statements about purposes and means in accounting according to a criterion of "cohesiveness" of the several statements?

GROUP 2. ON CHAMBERS' "BLUEPRINT"
AND THE CHAMBERS-LITTLETON EXCHANGE

1. Does Chambers' query on the conditions for an accounting theory assume the existence of a knower antecedent to what is known? How is this approach different from a modern behavioral approach? What is your reaction to the Dewey-Bentley thesis that knowings and knowns are dual aspects of the same transactions?

2. Does Chambers favor the application of the term "theory" to accounting rules of the type formulated in the Sanders-Hatfield-Moore *Statement of Accounting Principles?*

3. Under what criteria are the assumptions for an accounting theory to be selected, according to Chambers? Must the assumptions qualify under "relevance" and "fundamentalness" tests? Can "relevance" be taken to mean the relation of means to ends in view? Does Chambers frame propositions in terms of means-consequence patterns? Does he stress the isolation of "common elements" in observed particulars?

4. Does internal analysis suggest that Chambers' four assumptions are sense-data? Are they scientific refinements in terms of correspondence of change? Or are they conclusions about human motivations and purposes which themselves are subject to the conditions of inquiry? If the latter is the more appropriate interpretation, what is the sense in which Chambers uses the requirement of "fundamentalness"?

5. In his article "Choice among Alternatives" is Littleton suggesting that the conclusion comes first, and that "assumptions"

are then made to support the conclusions? Is that view consistent with the Littleton view in *Structure of Accounting Theory* that "experience" is the "given" element, and that "theory" consists in formulating appropriate "explanations" of "practice"?

6. Did Littleton make a fair selection of ideas from Chambers' article to represent Chambers' thesis? Do you think that Littleton's selection may have been determined by Littleton's own conception about conditions for validity of propositions?

7. Does Chambers continue the Littleton contrast between theory and practice, or does he integrate practice with theory as the experimentation phase of inquiry?

8. Chambers refers to a "series of methods" comprising "scientific method" as if the components of the series were independent modes of acquiring knowledge. Is the "scientific method" singular or plural; that is, can phases of inquiry of the order of "deduction" be identified operationally or only conceptually? Does your answer apply also to "induction"?

9. Does Chambers appear to be saying that relations among kinds, or existential propositions, can be determined by deductive reasoning? Attribution of that view to Chambers is supported by reference to Chambers' statement that "Reasoning leads to generalizations, principles and laws, the general body of which constitutes the science." Of course, there is a large element of indeterminacy in the phrase "leads to." Does Chambers ascribe the stated result to deductive elaboration of axioms?

10. Chambers contrasts scientific propositions with certain nonscientific propositions on the basis of the linguistic form of the statement. Identification is related to the use of the "indicative" versus the "imperative" mood. Does a hypothesis carry imperatives in the sense that it represents a directive for the selection and treatment of ideas and materials subject to testing by experimental operations? Can a hypothesis qualify as a scientific proposition if intermediary stages in the determination of warranted assertions are admissible?

11. Is Chambers' test for the validity of "scientific" propositions complete where the reference is limited to "its premises and its reasoning"?

12. In what sense is the term "value judgment" used by Chambers? Does Chambers' statement that a scientific proposition does not involve value judgments accord with the Dewey view?

13. Does Chambers assume that data are "given" in experi-

ence, and that the basic problem in applying the implications process is in selecting the right beginning data? How are the beginning data (the assumptions or axioms) known to be "right"? According to the degree of personal conviction that they reflect "reality"? Or, in addition, that the implicated propositions arrived at by deduction are also convincingly in accord with "reality"?

14. What is your appraisal of the realism of Chambers' four assumptions? Do they indicate behavior of persons on the order of traits identifying kinds of objects according to modes of interaction? Can a selection of axioms be made without regard to the consequences that are found to follow from their use?

15. Do the first two of Chambers' propositions represent analogies to biologic organisms? Different levels of organisms use different complexes of coordinating devices (that is, the definition of level); the "highest" levels of organisms anticipate consequences and regulate conduct in the light of the significance of the suggested means to desired consequences. Does Chambers use "rationality" in the sense of organization capacity?

16. Does Chambers' third proposition introduce an exchange economy as part of the picture of the environment in which the organisms operate? Is it the picture that needs are met through exchange, and not, say, through brute force; and that exchange involves, as an aspect of modern environment, the use of money as a medium of exchange and as a measure of value?

17. If the answers to the preceding several questions are affirmative, the accountant may be depicted under Chambers' fourth proposition as a specialized organism whose needs are met by offering for exchange certain services that can be utilized by other organisms to facilitate their satisfaction of needs in the environment of an exchange economy. Is the unique characteristic of the service offered by accountants, together with that of some other specialized organisms, the treatment of symbols or meanings as representative of existential data in the context of needs-satisfaction in an exchange economy?

18. Would an alternative set of propositions, based on (a) a conception of creation, (b) the faculty of reason, (c) revelation, and (d) sacrifice in helping other persons, be less "realistic" and therefore less suitable as starting assumptions for the implicatory process of deduction? Would the expectations of consequences flowing from the use of the alternative sets of propositions be a factor in their selection?

19. Are Chambers' starting propositions large in terms of numbers of devices accommodated as possibilities for aiding needs-satisfying organisms that follow the exchange mode for obtaining satisfactions? Is there any implicit limitation of techniques to, say, market-value accounting as contrasted with historical-cost accounting?

20. What distinction does Chambers intend by differentiating "basic propositions" from "axioms"? Are his "axioms" implicit in his four propositions, or are the axioms necessary expansions of the propositions to constitute refined statements of basic propositions? Are tests for the validity or suitability of "axioms" the same as for "propositions"? Does Chambers regard the "axioms" as "self-evident propositions" or as assumptions whose validity depends on the consequences following from their employment in inquiry?

21. Is Littleton's criticism ("Choice among Alternatives") of Chambers' "Blueprint" article largely a difference in opinion about appropriate assumptions? Does the criticism center on the conclusions? If conclusions are not deductively determined by assumptions, on what are the conclusions supported according to Littleton? What is the significance to Littleton of his assumption that the several "parts" of accountancy "are being welded into an integrated whole"?

22. Elaborate each of the following contentions: (a) Chambers asserts that theory "gives cohesion and consistency to practice"; (b) Littleton argues that the cohesiveness of accounting theory is a reflection of the "best" practice.

23. Can "scientific methods" be appropriately "applied" to "observable phenomena"? Or is the selection of data to constitute "phenomena" an integral part of the scientific method?

24. In what sense does Chambers require starting propositions to be "fruitful"? In the sense of providing corollaries that could be tested for consequences? In the sense that some associations with cultural life are included in the ordinary connotations of the terms employed? Or in some other sense?

GROUP 3.   ON "RESEARCH METHODOLOGY": DEVINE

1. In what sense or senses does Devine ("Research Methodology and Accounting Theory Formation") use the terms "logic" and "logical"? What features do "inductive logic" and whatever logic Devine contrasts with inductive logic have in common? Do you reserve the term "logic" for the organized study of the rules of deductive inference?

2. Does Devine emphasize symbolic logic in his reference to modern developments having social science significance?

3. Does Devine identify noninductive logic with the exploration of "requirements for a logical calculus"? May the term "mathematical system" be used interchangeably with "a logical calculus"? Is there a common core of meaning in the terms "logical calculus," "logical apparatus," "logical methods," "logical lines," and "logical rules"? Is there an emphasis on establishing the inferences among meanings within one or more meanings-systems, with the aid of symbolization in high degree?

4. Is Devine's message in the section on "logical structure and deductive systems" similar to that of Chambers, in respect to a needed emphasis on the deductive phase of inquiry among accountants? Does Chambers' exposition differ from that of Devine in respect to a distinction between an abstract and an "interpreted" deductive system? Or is the better terminology between a logical calculus and a deductive system? Would you use the term "model" as synonymous with a deductive (interpreted) system? Is it Devine's position that sometimes, but not always, an operative distinction between a logical calculus and an interpreted system can be maintained? What is the case in accounting?

5. Are Devine's illustrations from Littleton, Chambers, and Mattessich illustrations of the logical calculus or of the deductive system? Is the term "self-contained" superfluous in the phrase "self-contained deductive system"? Does Devine allege that Littleton developed *neither* a logical calculus or a deductive system? Or that Littleton, in the process of setting up definitions and classification categories, introduced the rudiments of a deductive system without appreciating the significance of his materials fully for such a system?

6. Does Devine identify the "postulational approach" with the development of a deductive system? Is the "rightness" or "wrongness" of a particular deductive system associated with the "realism" of the axioms and starting assumptions? Can the problem be stated as one of selecting the "correct" postulates? What criteria of correctness would you apply? The test of being "psychologically satisfying"? Would you regard the deductive system as a hypothesis, and require controlled experimentation as a condition for its warranted assertibility? Does Devine's requirement of "a reasonably accurate characterization" refer to a representation of interactions and processes? If so, is the test of adequacy of the

hypothesis or "theory" expressed in terms of reasonably anticipated consequences under specified conditions?

7. Is accounting merely "tinged with" or is it steeped in purpose? From the viewpoint of a mathematical purist, abstractions can be made from an accounting setting to accord with special purposes or aesthetics associated with logical calculus. From the viewpoint of processes of inquiry, accounting as a discipline is appropriately viewed instrumentally in its relation to ends in view.

8. Can you compare Devine's exposition of the scientific method with that of Dewey? Dewey sharply distinguishes conceptual and existential materials in inquiry; he does not make a strong contrast between "deductive" and "inductive" methods. There is, instead, a back-and-forth movement between the selection and ordering of data to serve as means and the framing of conceptions or hypotheses for guiding and directing the data selection and ordering. In what respects is this pattern different from Devine's presentation of an "interaction of deductive methods and the philosophical doctrine known as empiricism"?

9. Russell, whom Devine quotes approvingly, has been termed a "reductionist" in the sense that he relates the truth or falsity of a statement ultimately to certain nonverbal occurrences or empirical events experienced by individuals. A current spokesman for this view is generally taken to be A. J. Ayer, who is also quoted by Devine. Is it this reference of statements back to what Russell calls "factual premises" which Devine presents as "the philosophical doctrine known as empiricism"? If so, in what sense can it be said that this search for a "foundation" for scientific procedures interacts with deductive methods, or even that it is a component of scientific method?

10. How does Devine's position on "observation" compare with that of Dewey? Are objects taken to be "given" to experience? Are the conditions for effective observation better described in terms of breadth ("it is impossible to observe everything") or of depth (for example, one discriminates data from a qualitative situation in accordance with a controlling conception)? Can *any* set of data be obtained without abstracting from a more complete field of characteristics? In other words, is "abstraction" an identifiable stage of data treatment or is it an integral aspect of problem formulation?

11. Is Devine's statement that hypotheses "should have empirical import . . ." equivalent to his identification of a deductive

system as a logical calculus that has been "interpreted"? Does he emphasize the (deductive) drawing of implications?

12. According to Devine's meaning of "research method-ology," could the title of his article have been stated as "Scientific Method and Accounting Theory Formation"?

13. In your opinion, do the accounting doctrines expounded by Littleton rest on unsound behavior assumptions as suggested by Devine or are they based on certain philosophical predispositions, such as a predetermined unfolding of accounting activities according to a predestined pattern or the coherence value of doctrines in system?

14. Does Devine use the following terms with a common meaning: hypothesis with empirical content; deductive system; model? Is there a parallel relationship between model and behavioral act on the one hand, and social theory and precipitating event on the other? Is a behavioral hypothesis part of a model in the sense in which Devine uses the terms, or is the model limited to a set of static relationships? In either case, is the term "psychological" helpful in characterizing behavior traits, especially for use in disciplines other than psychology?

15. Can you state a frame of reference with respect to which a so-called "positivist view" has meaning? If "logical" means "implicated by deduction" (or "necessarily" related), in what sense can one "argue . . . logically on matters of fact"? Would you substitute "empirically" for "logically"? Or would you expand the meaning of logic to comprehend the theory of inquiry?

16. What criteria does Devine suggest for distinguishing between desirable and undesirable changes in customs and institutions? Can the accounting profession agree on the factors and degree of social change? Is Devine arguing that accountants should adopt, as a criterion for financial reporting, the promotion of socially desirable trends in institutions? And that this aim can be made effective only as accountants have developed warranted hypotheses about the effect of various patterns of financial reporting on the conduct of investors, creditors, labor unions, government, managers, and so forth?

17. Is Devine arguing that truth in financial reporting is determined by the practical consequences that are expected to follow from the reports? If so, how does his theory of truth compare with that of William James?

18. By what specific methods can the accountant relate ac-

counting-treatment rules for financial reporting to "existing social attitudes"? Is a willingness to use corporate financial reporting to influence income tax assessments an "existing social attitude"? If so, how should it influence the accountant's attitude toward the selection of accounting-treatment rules for financial reporting?

19. Can the inventory-pricing controversy be settled by applying the principle of adaptation to existing social attitudes? Where group interests are conflicting rather than complementary on a particular accounting question, are rules of weighting implied by "existing social attitudes"? Are there agreements about "hierarchies of worthiness" in the abstract, or are alignments of practical interest fluid and shaped by the mold of each concrete problem?

20. If empirical research discloses patterns of interest associated with sets of accounting-treatment rules, what *kinds* of factors should be referred to "the accepted social standard of the place and time"? Do the factors include the accountants' speculations about the feelings of justice that the various participants in the consequences will have toward the distribution of those consequences? Or the conformance of the "correct" accounting-treatment rules to statutory law and administrative regulation? Or concordance with "generally accepted principles of accounting"?

21. What is the ethical position of the accountant who selects accounting-treatment rules which are contrary to existing formalized law, on the ground that they are likely to induce actions which are consistent with an observed desirable trend of change in social institutions?

22. What evidence do you find in Devine's article that he regarded the four stated areas for comment as "interrelated"? Did he think of "research methodology" as equivalent to the scientific method, and did he see a direct applicability of the scientific method to accounting?

GROUP 4. ON "RESEARCH METHODOLOGY":
BEDFORD AND DOPUCH

1. Do Bedford and Dopuch criticize the Devine article for: (a) not presenting a comprehensive statement about accounting research in the sense of kinds of undertakings which they would designate research activities; or (b) for inadequately representing the scientific method; or (c) for not adopting some other criterion for warranted assertibility of propositions, such as Littleton's concept of "the nucleus of accounting theory"; or (d) for adopting the

Littleton concept under (c) but making statements inconsistent with it; or (e) for basically continuing the Littleton "core-function" concept, although in a modified form?

2. Do Bedford and Dopuch accept Littleton's "central purpose of accounting" as a premise for the development of their own proposal on an approach to accounting theory formulation? May that "central purpose" be stated as the determination and communication of indicators of efficient business operation? Or is the character of the indicators to be limited by particular "operational propositions" such as "realization, going concern, and costs attach"?

3. Does Littleton's formulation as presented by Bedford and Dopuch constrain inquiry by a requirement for the use of particular procedures independently of their establishment as suitable components of an indicator of business efficiency?

4. Do Bedford and Dopuch assert a need for removing Littleton's "central purpose" formulation as a "foundation" for accounting theory? Is the latter the gravamen of their criticism of Devine's position? Or do they agree on the need for a substitution, but differ on what change is desirable?

5. Do Bedford and Dopuch assert that Devine accepts certain restrictive procedural rules, such as costs attach or other predetermined rules, as implications of the latter's proposal for adapting accounting to the furtherance of changing objectives (selected as "worthy")?

6. Did Bedford and Dopuch say in effect that *even* under the current "structure" of accounting theory there are logically necessary relationships among the meanings of "functional objective, behavioral relations, and measurement"? And that these concepts and their interrelationships are employed in the Bedford-Dopuch formulation, whereas the Devine presentation fails to indicate the interrelationships?

7. What is the character of the interrelationships which Bedford and Dopuch assert exist among the meanings of "functional objective, behavioral relations, and measurement"? Do their several statements on this matter amount to a recognition of the central importance of the means-consequences relation in inquiry? Is the selection of data, including behavior traits and human interactions, dependent on the ends in view? Is the determination of quantitative relations among the existential materials of the inquiry an empirical process, so that measurement is an expression of the rules according to which unique measures of the particular materials are related?

8. Do Bedford and Dopuch reject the problem approach, involving choices between means-consequences patterns, as a basis for the selection of accounting-treatment rules in corporate financial reporting? Did they emphasize the interrelatedness of areas, on which Devine commented, for the purpose of demonstrating that the Devine proposal for adapting accounting methods to specified but changing objectives (majority objectives, or agreed objectives, or selected "social" objectives) was not *feasible?*

9. Which of the following points are included in the "lack of feasibility" argument of Bedford and Dopuch: (a) goal determination should be a prerogative of business management rather than of professional accountants; (b) at the present stage of accountants' capacities, they cannot determine either what majority goals are or what values are generally represented in specified goals; (c) accountants would be arrogating to themselves a function which is properly that of a Solomon were they to weigh and "balance" the desires and goals of various social groups; (d) behavior traits of persons affected by accountants' determinations are not sufficiently well established to serve as an element in a scientific hypothesis about the consequences of using alternative accounting-treatment rules in financial reporting; (e) even if behavior traits of classes of persons affected by financial reporting were warrantedly assertible in a probabilistic sense, the selection of one set of traits would necessarily submerge differences among classes of traits and variations within a class; (f) Devine emphasizes the anticipatory building of models and their impressment upon existential patterns of affairs, whereas the emphasis should be upon a determination of problem characteristics, and hypotheses should be closely tailored to the unique set of circumstances under consideration?

10. On what evidence in Devine's article can Bedford and Dopuch base their contention that Devine adopted any particular computational premise, such as the concept of realization in income measurement?

11. Do Bedford and Dopuch use the phrase "higher theories" in the sense of more general theories? Do you find any connotation of valuation in the use of the quoted phrase and the phrase "trivial theories"? Is there a scientific basis for an assertion that theories in all scientific fields will ultimately be generalized into a single theory that expresses the principle and order of Nature?

12. Which of the following two types of theories has been more often changed in the past: (a) "experimental laws" in the

sense of observed correlations, or (b) "theoretical laws" in the sense of hypotheses that attempt to connect observed uniformities into a more generalized description or "explanation" utilizing concepts of things that have not been observed? Do Bedford and Dopuch, borrowing from Kemeny, use the term "trivial theories" as equivalent to "experimental laws"?

13. Does the Bedford and Dopuch proposal dispense with the means-consequences relationship? Do these writers reject the relating of means to ends in view on the ground that the latter are numerous and varied? Do they propose that accounting concentrate on showing the existence, control, and utilization of economic goods over which particular firms have domination? Do they posit a lack of meaning for any data that are not associated with goal-directed activity? How does their thought framework differ from that of Devine?

14. May the Bedford-Dopuch article be interpreted as shifting attention, for accounting operations, from the traditional pattern of income measurement to change in value of economic resources as the criterion of business efficiency? Is the value-change concept implicit in the emphasis on scarcity of resources in relation to competing ends in view? Is this their essential point of difference with Devine, on the assumption that Devine adhered to the realization concept in determining the income-indicators of business efficiency? Will the importance of the problem of selecting the data that are appropriate to multiple goals be ameliorated if the accounting function is taken to be the reporting of "objective" changes in *market* values for those economic resources controlled by the particular firm?

15. Is the basic point of the Bedford-Dopuch difference with Devine that: (a) Bedford and Dopuch assume that Devine is continuing with the income concept as the principal tool for measuring economic efficiency for an organization, whereas (b) the joint authors recommend a *de novo* study of the organizational use of resources for the accomplishment of multi-goals? Do Bedford and Dopuch approach accounting through "organization theory"? Is the definition of "accounting" as a vocational area a secondary operation? (See Bedford, "Management Motives in Accounting Measurements," *Quarterly Review of Economics and Business*, Autumn 1963, pp. 35-45, for some financial reporting implications of the multi-goal approach to accounting.)

6

A Particular Framework
of Accounting Standards: Reflection
of the Cost-Allocation Doctrine

The readings assigned in connection with Chapter 3 of this syllabus pointed up an increasing recognition of the need for standards by which alternative accounting-treatment rules could be judged. The contemporary importance of such standards is associated with a broad public interest in the existence and operation of large business corporations, at least. The interests of one group may substantially correspond with the interests of other groups, or they may approximate a 180-degree opposition. The reconciliation of diverse interests may be taken as an end in view with respect to a determined problem. This is a philosophy of securities regulation, for example.

Even apart from governmental regulation, some reconciliation of diverse interests is essential to the continuity of the business entity. The institution of *contract* under legal sanction has long been recognized as an important mechanism for adjusting varying interests in society. Whether adjustments are based on agreement or on authority, there is a presumption that equitable alignments among diverse interests in a business entity are more likely to be achieved where the interests can be quantified and expressed in monetary terms. The question then posed to accountants is the character and scope of their participation in the reconciliation of interests function.

Accountancy as a profession has grown in correspondence with the recognition of need for a balancing of equities in the business and commercial world. Independence has become the key word in characterizing the distinctive function of the practicing professional accountant. Whether particular interests can be specified and weighted is a question on which Devine and Bedford and

Dopuch seemed to have some difference of opinion, as we have seen. But the classes of interests of special concern to accountants have been identified, and include at least stockholders, management, and creditors. There is, of course, a large shadow region between the kind "stockholders" and the kind "creditors." It is not clear that the contemporary classifications are operationally complete.

Under the philosophy of securities regulation, it does not appear that stockholders any more than other investors can reasonably rely upon corporate management to furnish them with complete and sound information about the progress and status of the corporation. The practicing professional accountant is an intermediary. The latter's opinions are expected to promote a fair, just, equitable, and sound adjustment of interests that may be in conflict.

The critical question faced by practicing professional accountants is whether their execution of the responsibilities of an intermediary in the equitable resolution of problems involves more than ethical requirements such as honesty and objectivity. The question that must be faced and answered is whether judgment about the *relevance* of data is a factor in the problem. If management discretion in reporting corporate status and results of activity needs to be constrained, *what* constraints should be imposed and *how* should the limitations be applied?

A current accounting issue is frequently represented in the literature as an opposition of *uniformity* and *flexibility*. A declared goal of the national organization of certified public accountants is the reduction of diversity of practices. Implementation processes employed to date have prominently included the force of *authority*. At this point we merely assert that the reference of accounting practices to standards is not avoided by authoritative declarations that only one out of a number of alternative accounting treatments shall be employed as the basis for an unqualified opinion. The declared proposition may become the standard of practice in an immediate sense, but the soundness of the declared treatment can be judged only by relating the standard practice to appropriate criteria.

In all social inquiry the consequences expected from particular policies and actions have a high degree of indefiniteness. Accounting propositions tend to receive intellectual acceptance mainly

on a showing of some analogical connection with simpler propositions that have already received a measure of acceptance. In our
opinion the postulational method will continue as a prominent
phase of the inquiry into accounting propositions. Much more can
be done, however, in the way of subjecting each postulate to re-
inquiry in regard to the bases for *its* acceptance. Most of all, we
need to recognize the tentative and hypothetical character of all
accounting propositions, to suspend *final* judgment indefinitely
while at the same time regarding a particular use of an accounting
rule as an additional opportunity for testing the hypothesis that directed the application of the rule, and to build case histories for
their suggestions of conditions under which one treatment appears
to be sounder than another.

The term "principles" continues to have a general utility in
identifying a conception that provides the rule for performing operations upon objects. A thing is determined to be one of a kind in
accordance with a "principle" of classification, and similarly kinds
are systematically related to other kinds. A general statement of
operations applicable to a set of symbols can appropriately be designated a "principle" on the basis of its generality. The student
should be on guard to distinguish the functional use of a "principle"
in inquiry from the notion of an insight into the "assumed" order
of Nature, intuited, and described as a "self-evident truth." You are
invited in following chapters of this syllabus to examine Accounting Research Studies No. 1 and No. 3 with this distinction in mind.

In the present chapter we shall examine the 1936 Statement
on corporate accounting standards prepared by the Executive Committee of the American Accounting Association. This Statement
was presented as representative of the best practice of the time. A
brief comparison of the 1936 Statement with the associated 1957
Statement is provided for in the study assignments. For a comparison of the four related Statements sponsored by the American Accounting Association, you are referred to a separate pamphlet by
the author (*The American Accounting Association-Sponsored Statements of Standards for Corporate Financial Reports, A Perspective*).

Major Propositions Constituting the 1936 Statement

Some degree of uncertainty about the elements of an accounting theory is indicated by the transformation in the title of the 1936 Statement as it passed through revisions in 1941, 1948, and most recently in 1957. In 1936 and in 1941 the content was labeled "principles"; in 1948 the designation was "concepts and standards"; and in 1957 the term "standards" was deemed sufficiently descriptive. The 1940 monograph by Paton and Littleton adopted the term "standards" for propositions of the kind represented in the 1936 Statement, and undertook to fabricate ("weave together") a structure of accounting theory which at least rationalized the standards presented in 1936.

Indications of the significance of a body of standards also underwent a change. Both the 1936 Statement and the 1941 Statement definitely referred the specific propositions to an unspecified "single (or unified) coordinated body of accounting theory." Referrals in the 1948 Statement and the 1957 Statement were made in more restrained language. Prefatory comments in the 1948 Statement seemed to emphasize the value of comparability through standardization, while resting on the somewhat implicit proposition that the character of the standards is determined by underlying conditions and purposes of accounting. It is interesting that the most recent Statement (1957) makes the least definite referral of the included propositions to an evaluation criterion. Reference is made to "conventions derived from experience," and to "concepts . . . underlying the conventions." Particular "concepts" are identified, as they were in 1948, but the relevance of concepts to any "body of accounting theory" is ignored.

The introduction to the 1936 Statement limits the application of the latter to corporate accounting, in connection with published reports of profit and financial position. It was thought that published financial statements cannot be interpreted by the "laymen," but should be understandable to "a person moderately experienced in business and finance." Such a person should be able to derive "the basic facts on which at least tentative business judgments may be premised." As a condition for the conveyance of information requisite to the formation of opinions on "condition and progress," the reports should be prepared under the guidance of operating rules with the properties of uniformity and clarity. Rules of this character could be designated "accounting principles."

The foregoing ideal had not at that time been realized completely. There was some degree of indefiniteness and lack of agreement on some "fundamental questions of principle." A consequence of the variations in practice was the noncomparability of information between corporate enterprises, and even between successive statements for a single enterprise. In such an environment businessmen who were so motivated could shape accounting results in the interest of expediency, supporting their positions with plausible and even persuasive arguments that had no foundation in logic. What was needed was agreement on ground rules, at least.

The committee claimed more than this for the particular rules it proposed. They were to be a "starting point" for a "comprehensive theory" of corporate financial reporting. The objective of the reporting was taken to be to communicate, especially to investors and creditors, accounting findings on the *utilization* of resources, and on some consequences for the "interests of" these two classes of persons.

Propositions about values were not necessarily relevant. Only those treatment rules which related to the "utilization" of resources and implications of the "utilization" for the "interests" of investors had to be considered. The emphasis, in the phrase "utilization of the economic resources" was on "utilization" and not on "economic." The fundamental premise which limited the suitability of deductively derived rules to serve as standards of practice was this: "Accounting is . . . not essentially a process of valuation, but the allocation of historical costs and revenues to the current and succeeding fiscal periods."

Twenty numbers are used to identify the "basic propositions of accounting," which are collected under three headings. There are almost equal numbers of propositions under each of the captions "costs and values," "measurement of income," and "capital and surplus." Despite the disclaimer that accounting is concerned with valuation, the Statement uses the term "valuation" to stand for the division of original cost between expired and deferred portions. No clues are given of the operations that would disclose either total "usefulness" or the portion "consumed, expired, or lost." One reviewer regarded the foregoing proposition, which he designated as Postulate No. 1, as reflecting the viewpoint of "certain of the owners." He suggested that *if* the committee chose to adhere to orthodox doctrine, the term "value" or "valuation" should be expunged. Thus the balance sheet would show "cost of future income, not the value of the corporation's future income." (Husband, "Accounting Postulates: An Analysis of the Tentative Statement of Accounting Principles," *The Accounting Review*, December 1937, p. 386.) He interpreted Postulate No. 1 as not permitting the use of lower-of-cost-or-market inventory method.

Proposition No. 2 centers on the concept of an entity. It says, in effect, that the original cost has a *value* significance in an economic sense when the factual context of a transaction justifies the interpretation that the transaction was a purchase rather than a pooling of interest. Scott ("The Tentative Statement of Principles," *The Accounting Review*, September 1937, p. 296) thought that the committee had not adequately defined "substantial change in ownership."

Proposition No. 3 has two parts. First, there is the statement that the propriety of particular cost allocations depends on future events, which must be forecast or "estimated." Second is a general consideration of criteria for estimating future events of the nature of "diminutions or expirations of cost." Operations whereby allocations made could be tested for their appropriateness are not specified, even in general terms. Development of particular practices toward this end are referred to "each enterprise and each industry." Scott regarded Point 3 as an elaboration of Point 1.

Proposition No. 4 does not deal with correct income determination or with its counterpart of unamortized cost, but with a social policy against correcting past errors by "reinstating" charged-off costs as assets except in correspondence with a correction of prior income statements. In Scott's opinion the purpose of the committee's recommendation was "to discourage manipulation." It was his view that good-faith mistakes should be correctible.

Proposition No. 5 is definitional, and concerns the breadth of the allocation or amortization concept. In Proposition No. 6 bond discount is classified as an offset against the face amount of the liability. Scott wondered whether the Statement was running to minutiae at this point; for him the proposition was wholly "unobjectionable."

Proposition No. 7 controls the manner in which "values other than unamortized costs" are to be shown in a position statement. They would come in only as supplementary information.

It is apparent that the principal propositions in the section on "costs and values" are expansions of the beginning *assumption* made by the committee: that "accounting is . . . the allocation of historical costs." That proposition and its corollaries are thought to provide *definiteness* in the interest of *uniformity*. Yet in their application there should be *flexibility*. The authors did not provide criteria for determining the areas for, or the extent of, variation, except by presenting a moral admonition that "legitimate" needs should be provided for under "all ordinary circumstances." Negatively, the authors rejected experienced changes in purchasing power or money as a basis for deviation from the application of the historical-cost standard.

In one respect, however, the stated propositions may include a doctrine which is not consistent with the premise that historical cost should be divided between the portion expired and an unexpired portion to be carried forward. For example, Husband thought that Proposition No. 1 carried the implication that inventory could not be priced at lower-of-cost-or-market. The semantic route traveled by the committee was to utilize a doctrine of cost absorption to meet the difficulty later observed by Husband. The carrying value of assets was to be reduced to "such amounts as may reasonably be expected to be recoverable in the course of future operations"; this guide was applicable to "assets in use or ultimately to be marketed," and might be deemed to apply to plant assets as well as to inventories.

Six propositions comprise a "measurement of income" set. It was the opinion of Scott that the Statement did "not define income except by inference. . . . By implication, income is made to include all gains except those arising out of dealings with the corporation's own stockholders."

Proposition No. 8 presents the viewpoint of the "all-inclusive Income Statement." All revenues "properly" recognized *within a particular period* and all costs written off *in that period* should be included in the *Income Statement for that period*. The goal sought was the complete representation of income items in the *series* of Income Statements. You may recall that the Accounting Procedure Committee of the American Institute of Accountants preferred to have the Income Statement shaped by the "operating performance" doctrine. The Securities and Exchange Commission's solution of the problem interpreted the issue as one involving the form of presentation.

The possibility of two sections in an Income Statement was recognized in Proposition No. 9. The separation involved an interpretation of the category of "operations." Identification of major components of each of the two sections was the burden of Propositions No. 10 and No. 11. The operations section included "income and profits taxes accrued," and in general was intended to reflect "normally recurring" items. The second section of the Income Statement was residual; the committee did indicate types of items to be placed there, mainly under the descriptions of "capital" or "extraordinary." Proposition No. 12 provided a negative condition for the determination of net income: profits or losses on dealings with the corporation's stockholders were to be excluded from income, as was also any "adjustment of the capital accounts."

Proposition No. 4 had prohibited the "reinstatement" of costs previously charged off, except under one condition. Proposition No. 13 implements that exception and specifies the procedure under which publication of corrections of prior Income Statements should be made.

It thus appears that the six propositions labeled "measurement of income" do not introduce any operative criteria that either modify or implement the basic *assumption* of cost allocation or the reflection of that assumption in Proposition No. 1. The concept of "income" implied in the propositions is delineated only at the margin of dealings with stockholders. The most important concept in this set of propositions is the "all-inclusive Income Statement" notion. Recognition is given to the possibility of distinguishing "operating" and other transaction effects. It was thought essential that both results be summed and presented as a single net income figure for the reason that the pattern of financial reporting in the United States featured "per share" results in the singular. If currently recognized events relating to operations of prior years were likely to lead to misinterpretation of currently reported results, recourse

could be had to the option of presenting revised Income Statements along with the current Income Statement. A condition for
intelligent comparison of Income Statements in a series was that
"operating reserves" should not be used where their effect is the
"distortion" or "artificial stabilization" of income.

Seven propositions are grouped under the heading "capital
and surplus." Proposition No. 14 defines "the capital of a corporation" as consisting of "paid-in capital and earned surplus." The concept of paid-in capital is expanded by Propositions No. 15, 16, and
17. Proposition No. 15 recognizes, as components of paid-in capital,
amounts transferred from earned surplus in connection with stock
dividends or recapitalizations. Proposition No. 16 recognizes a
Limbo status for reacquired shares that may be reissued; as to other
reacquired shares, any excess of acquisition price over a pro-rata
portion of capital stock and paid-in surplus was a charge against
earned surplus. Proposition No. 17 contains a restrictive provision
that no losses should be charged against paid-in surplus; nor should
losses be charged against the reserves component of earned surplus,
but should affect earned surplus only through "the income account."

Earned surplus is the subject of Propositions No. 18 and 19. A
restrictive list of charges or credits to earned surplus is provided.
The basic element is the amount of income periodically determined.
Proper treatment of the excess of acquisition price of reacquired
shares, previously set out in Proposition No. 16, is restated in the
proposition on earned surplus. Changes in surplus reserves are to
wash through the earned surplus account. A negative precept is
furnished, against crediting earned surplus in connection with the
reacquisition of the corporation's shares. Husband noted that Proposition No. 19 seems to expand Proposition No. 15; after a reduction of par value or stated value of capital stock to absorb a deficit,
or where a deficit is transferred to paid-in surplus, earned surplus
must be dated. The concluding proposition deals with disclosure
of changes in capital stock and surplus in periodic reports.

The authors' justificatory comments for the last set of propositions indirectly raised the issue of a possible conflict between reporting on the utilization of resources in terms of its implications
for investors' interests, and reflecting legal requirements, in a single
set of financial reports. The ideal for reporting in the capital-and-

surplus area was to contrast (1) changes in contributed capital and (2) changes in stockholders' equity due to all other influences except "stock transactions with stockholders." (We have seen that earned surplus was to be reduced, but could not be increased, by differences between acquisition price of reacquired shares and pro-rata portions of capital stock and paid-in surplus; the reduction was interpreted as a "distribution" of earned surplus.)

The 1936 Statement brought a considerable response in the accounting literature. Articles commenting on this Statement prior to 1940 are listed in the bibliography of the Paton and Littleton monograph. Apart from recommendations in the 1936 Statement for the classification and reporting of items by categories in the Income Statement and Balance Sheet, what basic propositions do you find in the Statement in addition to the committee's starting *assumption* that "accounting is . . . a process of . . . the allocation of historical cost . . ."? Do you find in the Statement a rationale for the recommendations? To provide such a rationale was the express purpose of the Paton and Littleton monograph.

READINGS

"Tentative Statement of Principles Affecting Corporate Reports," *The Accounting Review,* June 1936, pp. 187-191. The document is also available in a pamphlet of collected Statements published by the American Accounting Association.

SCOTT, DR, "The Tentative Statement of Principles," *The Accounting Review,* September 1937, pp. 296-303.

HUSBAND, GEORGE R., "Accounting Postulates: An Analysis of the Tentative Statement of Accounting Principles," *The Accounting Review,* December 1937, pp. 386-401.

"Concepts and Standards Underlying Corporate Financial Reports, 1957," *The Accounting Review,* October 1957, pp. 536-546. This document is also available in the pamphlet referred to above.

STAUBUS, GEORGE J., "Comments on Accounting and Reporting Standards for Corporate Financial Statements—1957 Revision," *The Accounting Review,* January 1958, pp. 11-24. Study of the sections on income determination is especially recommended.

QUESTIONS

1. Can the characterization of the 1936 Statement as a "model" (Dein, "A Glance Backward at Research in Accounting," *The Accounting Review*, January 1961, pp. 1-8) be reconciled with its characterization as "an accountants' creed" (Husband, "Accounting Postulates: An Analysis of the Tentative Statement of Accounting Principles," *The Accounting Review*, December 1937, p. 401)?

2. Is the accountants' intermediary function in the reconciliation of interests satisfied by presenting data that *may* be relevant to diverse business and financial problems constituting an "open-end" list? Does their function include the specific appraisal of a management's actions for the enlightenment of an identified class of interested persons such as stockholders or long-term creditors? If accountants do have the latter responsibility, is a choice between cost allocation and value-change measurement relevant for its execution? Can that responsibility be satisfied by presenting alternative indices under the general pattern of Husband's three-part Income Statement?

3. Does the accountant have a responsibility for indicating the earning power of the business reported on? Is earning power indicated by the trend of net income figures developed under the cost-allocation premise? Is income tax allocation supportable on the ground that such allocation is necessary in order that the trend of *before*-tax profits is not changed by income tax charges?

4. How is the realization doctrine related to the cost-allocation function of accounting for income reporting?

5. Can you state a hypothesis in which the "costs attach" fiction is a part? What is the relation of that fiction to the requirement that a hypothesis be capable of directing operations that will provide data that can serve to test the hypothesis of which the fiction is a part?

6. Do you agree that a major function of accounting services is the "protection of equities"? How is the choice of income-calculation rules related to the performance of such a function?

7. Is the question of management discretion in reporting corporate status and results of activity a currently critical one for accountants? What limitations on managements' choices of accounting-treatment rules did the May Committee recommend in 1932? Was the 1936 Statement sponsored by the American Accounting

Association intended to restrict management choice further than the May Committee's recommendation would have done? Was there a common requirement that accounting rules should express the assumption that accounting is a process of cost allocation?

8. How would you expand the proposition that avoidance of direct regulation of corporate accounting and reporting for large public corporations depends upon satisfactory performance by the public accounting profession?

9. Are "uniformity" and "flexibility" of accounting and reporting standards precise and contradictory terms?

10. Is the individual accountant able to demonstrate the soundness of his conclusions in a particular case without resort to a "framework of authoritative concepts and standards"?

7

Elaboration
of the Cost-Allocation Doctrine:
Contemporary Accounting "Theory"

For the most part the accounting theory exposited by Paton and Littleton in *An Introduction to Corporate Accounting Standards* is a theory of accounting practice. That is, the standards comprising the 1936 Statement represent organized generalizations of practices recognized as desirable by leaders in the practicing area of accounting; these were designated by Kohler "the best standards of the day" ("Why Not Retain Historical Cost?", *Journal of Accountancy*, October 1963, p. 35). Differences between the American Accounting Association Committee standards and recommendations of the American Institute of Accountants' Committee on Accounting Procedure or the Securities and Exchange Commission may be noted in context. We have observed, however, that the latter committee employed an ad hoc approach and did not generally show the relationship of its conclusions to any organized body of propositions. Thus positive and negative considerations combine to support our emphasis on the Paton and Littleton monograph for analysis and appraisal. The latter document has had broad acceptance since its publication in 1940.

In the present chapter we shall probe for clues to philosophical considerations that may have influenced Paton and Littleton to formulate tests for accounting standards in the way they did, and we shall note the dependence of most current proposals for price-level adjustments on the doctrine that accounting is a process of cost allocation.

The Paton and Littleton Exposition
of Accounting Theory

The authors of *An Introduction to Corporate Accounting Standards* do not present a succinct set of propositions labeled "the accounting theory." The bulk of the relevant considerations may be gleaned from the first two chapters, on "standards" and on "concepts." The subsequent four chapters of the monograph expand the fundamental notions, under the captions of "cost," "revenue," "income," and "surplus." In the final chapter, labeled "interpretation," the authors consider some proposals for extending information beyond that derived from the conventional framework of accounts which reflect their theory of accounting. On the whole the authors' position is that the several sallies into the domain of conventional accounting should be strictly contained.

In their introduction to Chapter I on standards, Paton and Littleton emphasize a need for "a consistent framework of standards." And in the body of that chapter the authors set out their views on conditions which standards must meet in order for sound results to follow from their use. Their summary statement is, "Thus accounting standards should be orderly, systematic, coherent; they should be in harmony with observable, objective conditions; they should be impersonal and impartial." Other tests are stated in connection with a survey of considerations leading up to the quoted observation.

The foregoing general criteria for standards seem to be consistent, in part, with standards for inquiry developed earlier in this syllabus. There is a basis for an impression, however, that a rationalistic philosophy has guided the formulation. At another point the authors say, "A statement of accounting standards should represent an integrated conception of the function of accounting as a means of expressing the financial facts of business in a significant manner."

The meaning of "integrated conception" is not clearly conveyed in the monograph. Is the meaning the same as accordance with "the accepted hallmarks of clear thinking"? Is the requirement that accounting standards be "definite, meaningful, and widely applicable" a different kind of requirement than "integrated conception" or a product of "clear thinking"? Is there any inconsistency between the requirements that standards (a) must be expressed as generalized propositions on "fundamental conceptions and general approaches to the presentation of accounting facts" and (b) must be "definite, meaningful, and widely applicable"? If accounting propositions are assumed to reflect the order of Nature, and if Nature is a unity constructed on a building-block principle, then the two conditions expressed by the authors might be expected to coalesce. The authors specify also that ". . . standards should represent . . . [a] conception . . ." Later they add the requirements of "relevance" and "groundedness" for accounting standards. Throughout the discussion the authors write in anatomic rather than operational terms.

Paton and Littleton seem to use the terms "concept" and "proposition" interchangeably. The following "concepts" are identified by the authors: business entity; continuity of activity; measured consideration; costs attach; effort and accomplishment; and verifiable, objective evidence. Our suggestion is that the reader state propositions which are associated with each of the concepts noted and indicate connections expressly asserted or implied by the authors for the several propositions.

The four major propositions advanced by Chambers ("Blueprint for a Theory of Accounting," *Accounting Research,* 1955, pp. 17-25) may be reviewed in comparison with the Paton and Littleton propositions.

The business entity

Did Paton and Littleton chart their passage from the simple *concept* of business entity to a *proposition* about costs and assets? They say, "With the entity concept as a basis, there is no difficulty in accepting the proposition that all costs legitimately incurred by the enterprise are properly included, in the first instance, in the total of assets." The legitimacy restriction seems to have no close connection with the entity notion. More importantly, the identification of an entity carries no implication of a restriction to cost measurements as contrasted with value measurements. Are the authors here anticipating their presentation of the notion that "costs attach"?

The entity or enterprise notion is quite general. It permits the adoption of one of a number of points of view. For example, wages may be regarded as either a cost or as a distribution of enterprise income. A usual interpretation of the enterprise merges contractual and residual investors and contrasts that amalgam with the providers of personal services. On page 9 of their monograph Paton and Littleton specify "enterprise asset-changes" as the subject-matter of accounting theory.

One view of a scientific proposition is that it is capable of directing operations. Emphasis is placed not on "existences," but on consequences of interactions. Many propositions in accounting literature fail to satisfy the foregoing condition. Paton and Littleton state: "If the corporation were viewed as merely an aggregation of individual investors, it would be consistent to hold that the earnings of the enterprise belonged to the investors from the moment of original realization." Is the entity concept employed by the authors here capable of directing operations with the purpose of testing the validity of the "belongingness" proposition?

The second clause of the sentence quoted in the preceding paragraph does not necessarily follow from the first clause. It does not rule out other viewpoints on the relation of investors to measures of corporate assets. A new stockholder probably views all of his expenditure for shares as an investment of capital, independently of the source of the present resources of the entity. From the viewpoint of the "aggregation" it is doubtful that the distinction between "capital" and "accumulated earnings" is relevant.

Identification of an entity can be influenced by the adoption of a doctrine of "pooling of interest." Is a standard that recognizes a distinction between "pooling of interest" and "purchase" in harmony with "observable, objective conditions"? Consideration of the preceding distinction raises the issue of the influence that "intention" or purpose of the "entity directors" should have in the shaping of accounting standards.

Apparently the choice between an entity or an aggregate point of view is not crucial. According to Husband ("The Corporate-Entity Fiction and Accounting Theory," *The Accounting Review*, September 1938, pp. 241-253), "Both the entity and representative viewpoints are capable of supporting a coherent body of accounting theory." One would ask whether one body of theory would be more realistic than the other, or more effective in guiding operations to yield data that would test the theory. Points of view of "equity" and "residual equity" have also been distinguished (Staubus, "The Residual Equity Point of View in Accounting," *The Accounting Review*, January 1959, pp. 3-13).

It is possible that the significance of the entity concept would be enhanced by a determination of the activities and relations of the "firm." The problem would then be to determine the criteria that should be applied to segment the activities and position of a unit in an inter-related business complex. This kind of analysis suggests some emphasis to the experimental over the deductive phase of inquiry (Ives, "The Nature of the Accounting Unit," *The Accounting Review*, October 1951, pp. 516-517).

In the same vein, fund-flow analyses and cash-flow analyses may be more objective tools than income measurement, in relation to decisions and actions of the enterprise.

Many textbooks have followed the practice of identifying accounting "theory" with an elaboration of selected "concepts." Among the many treatments of the entity notion is Chambers' first proposition in the latter's "Blueprint" article.

Continuity of activity

Chambers' second proposition posited rational action toward fulfillment of the income objective. Continuity of corporate life was deemed to be a condition rather than a fundamental accounting proposition.

Paton and Littleton seem to use the notion of "continuity of activity" as a building block in a structure of ideas whose acceptability is indicated by its degree of orderliness, systematization, and coherence. There are the suggestions that *form* is the reality and that knowledge of the world can best be apprehended by abstracting and combining observed forms. Their term "integrated conception" contributes to the preceding interpretation.

Can you state the basic Paton and Littleton *proposition* that is associated with the continuity of activity concept? Is the proposition simply that continuity of life is the normal expectation for a business entity? Is the "continuity of activity" concept coextensive with the "going-concern" assumption? If a statistical approach showed a high rate of business failures and liquidations, one would expect some modification of the assumption that an enterprise will continue indefinitely. But the ultimate need of testing the validity of the proposition as a basis for accounting treatments would remain.

It may be that the going-concern outlook is a practical condition of the attempt to compare effort with accomplishment for modern industrial firms. According to Paton and Littleton, periodic financial reports are a practical necessity in an environment where "the complete picture of an enterprise is never entirely discernible prior to final liquidation." One wonders, however, about the meaning of "provisional" reports in a situation where *no* liquidation date for the enterprise is assumed. Where managerial facilities are applied to changing products, the enterprise can continue despite obsolescence of particular products. Possibly the term "final liquidation" should refer to the exhaustion of specific items of real capital. From the enterprise viewpoint, however, the composition of real capital continuously changes (in a series of discrete changes) within a continuing large (modern) corporation. "Provisional estimates" are tested, not by values at the date of an (assumed) liquidation of an enterprise, but by subsequent events *within* the life of a *continuing* enterprise.

The authors are emphatic in asserting that "earning power not cost price, not replacement price, not sale or liquidation price —is the significant basis of enterprise value." They indicate that the foregoing proposition is "strengthened," not merely reflected or exhibited by the "concept of continuity." Yet earning power looks to the future, while the accountants' Income Statement is taken to represent the results of past events. Therefore the statement that the Income Statement exhibits "management's effectiveness in handling the available resources" cannot be a logical deduction (*sequitur*) from the "earning power" proposition.

Looking at the authors' statement of the function of the Income Statement independently of the "earning power" proposition, there are concepts and processes underlying the Income Statement that interfere with the implementation of the stated objective, that is, to exhibit "management's effectiveness in handling the available resources." Market changes are not within the control of the typical management. Nor is management responsible for changing price levels. Even within the framework of business-determined events, a particular Income Statement reflects the effects of management decisions made in other income periods. Of course, the foregoing limitations of the Income Statement as an exhibit of management's effectiveness are not removed by the presentation of a connected series of Income Statements that includes all "special and nonrecurring losses and gains."

In particular, the continuity postulate does *not* require emphasis on costs instead of values. An emphasis on values and valuation is quite compatible with the continuity concept. Restated, the accountant does *not* "emphasize the flow of costs and the interpretation of assets as balances of unamortized costs" *because* of the accountant's concern with "the administration of the affairs of the continuing business institution."

We have noted the 1936 Statement's adoption of an assumption that accounting is concerned with the allocation of costs. This proposition was assumed, not demonstrated as either necessary or sound. The Paton and Littleton monograph continues the assumption that "truthful and significant measurements" of income are dependent on the "allocation of costs and revenues as between the present and future."

One argument frequently advanced in support of the cost-allocation premise is that it is the only approach that conforms to an asserted "objectivity" requirement. In following paragraphs of this syllabus we shall see how Paton and Littleton attempt to provide another basis of support for the cost-allocation doctrine. At this point you should review the relation of the "realization" doctrine to the cost-allocation assumption.

Measured consideration

The third of Chambers' four propositions relates to the usefulness of statements expressed in monetary terms for rational conduct in pursuit of the income objective. The Paton and Littleton proposition is more restricted: "The basic subject matter of accounting is . . . the measured consideration involved in exchange activities . . ." "Measured consideration" is here also called "price aggregate," and in purchase situations it is identified with "cost," or ". . . transactions re-expressed quantitatively as price aggregates for the purpose of accounting."

The term "transaction" does not have a single obvious meaning. What transactions are is determined by the accountants' selection rules. The term as generally used in accounting includes such disparate considerations as money exchanges, cost conversions as in inventory-tracing, and the assignment of costs as expenses in depreciation accounting. An issue frequently presented in the literature is whether the accountant elects his transactions from the whole of business data more in accordance with the principle of "significance" or of "objectivity." The nondescriptive term "imponderables" is often used to refer to an open-ended region of "nonaccounting" data.

What is your reaction to the following interpretation of the function that Paton and Littleton accord to "price-aggregates"? It is the authors' position that, since the accountant undertakes to *relate* business data which he selects, he must express the data in "homogeneous terms." The common denominator that the authors designate for expressing exchange transactions is the "measured consideration," which, in most transactions with outsiders, is identical with the "price aggregate." The accountant must express his data in homogeneous terms because he will perform mathematical operations upon the data. It is important that both revenues and costs be expressed in homogeneous terms for the purposes of the mathematical operations that will be applied to these quantities. The homogeneity is obtained by assigning to revenues and costs a common name, "price aggregate." An alternative to the conclusion expressed in the preceding sentence is that the common denominator of exchange transactions is "service potential" rather than the merely convenient "price aggregate." A second alternative is that price aggregate has significance at the time of acquisition of the associated item because it expresses "value," or a ratio of significance to all other economic goods, *at that time.*

Costs attach

The authors have elevated an aspect of the "matching" concept (the association of costs and revenues as indicators of effort and accomplishment) to a basic proposition controlling accounting methodology. The authors assert that "accounting assumes that acquisition costs are mobile and may be apportioned or regrouped, and that costs reassembled have a natural affinity for each other which identifies them with the group." The authors clearly state the costs attach notion as an "as if" proposition. But a lack of correspondence to reality does not necessarily require its abandonment.

Fictions have a recognized functional position in inquiry. (You may be interested in reading Vaihinger, *The Philosophy of As-If.*) The critical question is, what distinguishes fiction from fantasy? A fiction is chosen with reference to its suitability as a means in attaining some end in view. And its suitability must be tested by its fruitfulness in directing operations providing the data that serve to test the hypothesis of which the fiction is a part. Thus the costs-attach fiction must be accepted tentatively rather than finally. It apparently has served businessmen as a control device. Is it also useful for the determination of periodic income?

The authors' distinction between "cost of production" and "value" appears to be based on an assumption that the enterprise makes a single product, and that all costs are product costs rather than period costs. Otherwise the sale of product could not be expected to establish the difference between cost of production and value. This dilemma might be avoided by negating a reconciliation between cost of production and value, and asserting merely that regrouped costs "express parts of the total effort made to bring about a subsequent advantageous sale." The denial that the regrouped costs approximate a partial expression of value would permit the authors to introduce the fact that not all costs are associated with product, but that some are treated as period costs.

The term "recapture of costs" introduces confusion into the analysis. Users of this term do not assign any operational meaning to it, but use it in the sense of identifying a mathematical difference between an aggregate of revenues and an aggregate of associated costs.

Enterprise effort and accomplishment

In Littleton's reply ("Choice among Alternatives," *The Accounting Review*, July 1956) to Chambers' proposal of a starting point for formulation of an accounting theory ("Blueprint for a Theory of Accounting," *Accounting Research*, January 1955), the joint author of the Paton and Littleton monograph alluded to the importance of "the central and controlling characteristic of accounting." The meaning of that phrase was not evident to Chambers in the latter's rebuttal ("Detail for a Blueprint," *The Accounting Review*, April 1957) of Littleton's criticism. Its meaning is suggested by Littleton's emphasis elsewhere (*Structure of Accounting Theory*) on "enterprise effort and accomplishment" as the most important of four "principles . . . expressive of the central purpose of accounting." The term "matching" has come to be used as a short symbol for the same notion.

Paton and Littleton state the related proposition as follows: "The ideal is to match costs incurred with the effects attributable to, or significantly related to, such costs." In effect they are referring to an assumed functional relationship between costs and revenues. Unfortunately for the implementation phase, economic statisticians have had very limited success in arriving at statistical cost functions, even in the short run.

Some of the problems can be seen when the matching proposition is deductively explored. The content of the cost concept will vary with the purpose for which its use is directed (planning changes in the plant structure; evaluating past investment decisions) and with the conditions under which activities are carried on or contemplated. The cost concept is not rigidly determined by the notion of "measured consideration." If an item of plant or equipment is not currently used in fashioning a product sold during a period, some premise must be sought for making a related cost charge against current revenue. More generally, revenues may be associated with a whole complex of factors, some of which are external to the firm. The specific contribution of particular cost factors cannot be determined directly. And much tenuous reasoning has been resorted to in attempts to demonstrate degrees of indirect relationship.

Dissatisfaction with "full cost" reasoning has prompted some accountants to advocate emphasis on contributions accounting in managerial decision-making. And the notion of variable costing is currently being urged for inventory pricing for the purposes of published financial statements.

If the premise is adopted that income accounting, with the corollary of matching of costs with revenues, is a desirable goal, the issue is presented of the criteria for associating costs with revenues. This question of course opens up a major part of the accounting-standards problem, which is discussed throughout this and other accounting courses. Mention of the problem at this point is designed to re-emphasize the need for search into the bases for accounting practices.

Verifiable, objective evidence

The authors here state a generalization from observations, that professional auditors have continued to emphasize "objective evidence" in connection with their professional task of "verifying transactions." The exemplary classes of transactions cited by the authors are sales and expenditures. On the basis of the foregoing observation and an additional observation on the complexity of business activities and the increased remoteness of investors from management, the authors conclude: "Verifiable, objective evidence has . . . become . . . a necessary adjunct to the proper execution of the accounting function of supplying dependable information." Evidence that is "objective" is defined as evidence that is "impersonal and external to the person most concerned, in contrast with that person's unsupported opinion or desire."

At this point in their discussion of the "basic concepts or assumptions underlying accounting" the authors attempt to relate their analysis to their conception of the scientific method. Their interpretation of the latter process emphasizes "objectively determined facts," and ascribes a "complete and conclusive objectivity" to "completely scientific" data.

In our view objects are selected as facts on the basis of their potential for resolving an unsettled situation and on the basis of their operability under a controlling, directive hypothesis. Facts are not given independently of inquiry. While objects can have different degrees of warrantability, complete certainty does not attach to any proposition about the real world. Apparently the authors recognize that the use of the scientific method is not unique to the investigation of physical phenomena, but that it can be applied in the social sciences to yield propositions with varying degrees of warrantedness.

Summary

The accounting "theory" advanced by Paton and Littleton to support the propositions constituting the 1936 Statement seems to be a combination of selected implications from a few "underlying concepts," molded in a way that might be expected to add credence to the basic assumption on which the 1936 Statement was based: accounting is a process of allocation of cost.

It was our opinion that the "business entity" concept is at least neutral with respect to a choice between cost allocation and value-change measurement, and that the latter is just as consistent with a "continuity of activity" concept as is the former.

The doctrine of "measured consideration" derives its significance from a value context. The choice of a cost label for the exchange value does not add significance. The authors might have elected to justify the ascription of a continuing economic importance to the price aggregate by using arguments associated with the classical "cost theory of value," or theory of long-run determination of price through dominance of the cost of production influence. In Paton's 1922 book on *Accounting Theory,* that author did note a cost theory of value as a possible reference for the accountants' cost concept. The authors of the monograph elected instead to assert that costs were at all times comparable with revenues because homogeneity had been effected through the identification of cost with value in exchange at the acquisition date.

The doctrine that "costs attach" is in part a corollary of the proposition that price aggregate has economic significance at dates subsequent to the acquisition date. In addition it involves the adoption of a notion analogous to "embodied service potential." Costs can be peeled off in measured amounts, or faggots of service can be removed from a bundle in discrete pieces, in meaningful association with revenues. In our opinion the usefulness of this common fiction for income determination must be tested by reference to independent measurements of value changes.

Finally, the doctrine that accounting can concern itself only with objective data contains implications both for the participation of non-accountants in providing aids to decision-making and for the selection of data meeting the accounting standard of objectivity. On the latter point, Paton and Littleton's meaning of "objective" can be commended, as it indicates the need for evidence in support of opinions. We shall see in Chapter 9 of this syllabus that Sprouse and Moonitz also rely on a doctrine of objectivity of data to support their recommendation, in Accounting Research Study No. 3, for the employment of market valuations in some cases.

We conclude that Paton and Littleton did not provide any general theory of accounting, in the sense of an integrated meanings-system in correspondence with a classification system for objects by kinds in terms of interactions. They did not provide a hypothesis about consequences which might be expected from the employment of particular accounting-treatment rules, even in the area of public business corporations. Were they expected to perform this type of task? Did the program under which the Accounting Principles Board was created set out a similar objective? Can a general theory of accounting be formulated in advance of special theories?

Price-level Adjustment as a Refinement of the Cost-Allocation Doctrine

The assumption that income determination is based on the performance of operations upon historical cost pervades the several Statements from 1936 to 1957, and the Paton and Littleton monograph. The 1957 Statement introduced a current-cost standard for the treatment of inventories; this was an outstanding exception. Each of the Statements did recognize the principle of invalidation of accounting income through extensive price-level movements. Not before the issuance of Supplementary Statement No. 2 (supplementing the 1948 Statement) in 1951 were the experienced changes in average price deemed extensive enough to be significant. The conclusion that special reporting for price-level changes may be desirable was strengthened to a mandatory reporting requirement in the 1957 Statement. However, the special reporting was only supplementary to the main stream of reporting based on historical cost. The door had been opened but the screen was still in place.

Publication of Supplementary Statement No. 2 in August, 1951, was followed shortly by two review articles authored by individual members of the Association's committee. In January, 1952, Hill published an "analysis and interpretation of the discussions and conclusions of the group" ("An Analysis of Supplementary Statement No. 2," *The Accounting Review*, January 1952, pp. 16-24). In the same month Maurice Stans, "the only member of that committee who is engaged in public accounting practice," published an analysis of "the conclusions of the group" ("AAA Proposals Offer Practical Suggestions for Dealing with Price Level Changes in Accounting," *Journal of Accountancy*, January 1952, pp. 52–59). Thus communication was prompt to both academic and practicing accountants. Each of the articles referred to the other.

The 1951 document was a plea for open-mindedness in experimentation on the adjustment of accounting data for price-level changes, subject to the restriction that historical-cost accounting should be changed, if at all, only by refining the measuring unit. As Stans cautioned, "The statement *does not endorse* the adjusted cost concept as a present or future standard or requisite for accounting reports. It calls for evidence of the usefulness . . . and waits upon such evidence . . ." The committee's adherence to the historical-cost premise is also pointed up in Stans' interpretation that a deductive conclusion from the committee's recommendation is that "LIFO should be eliminated as a historical cost procedure in favor of FIFO."

Apparently Stans concentrated on the conclusion of the committee. Hill's article pointed up some problems of acceptance raised within the committee in the process of reaching the compromise conclusion.

The American Accounting Association had earlier used an experimental approach to the price-level adjustment question. Under the guidance of Ralph C. Jones, mechanisms of adjustment had been applied to the historical-cost data for four companies, and the results were evaluated in Jones, *Effects of Price Level Changes on Business Income, Capital and Taxes.* Professor Jones was also a member of a project advisory committee sponsored by the American Institute of Certified Public Accountants which guided a careful study of price-level adjustment techniques and issues. The latter study report, prepared by the Staff of the Accounting Research Division of the Institute, was published as Accounting Research Study No. 6 in 1963. The study recommendation that price-level-adjusted financial statements be used to supplement rather than replace unadjusted statements was related by the study group to an assumption that the present and the near future constitute "a period of education, experimentation, and transition."

In striking contrast to the reservation of judgment on price-level adjustment methods until the consequences of their use can be assessed is the emotive adherence to a previously accepted position, as well as the assertion of finality for a conclusion reached on predominantly deductive grounds.

An interesting exercise in the analysis of arguments is presented by an interchange of articles between Dein ("Price-Level Adjustments: Fetish in Accounting," *The Accounting Review*, January 1955, pp. 3–24) and Husband ("Professor Dein, Mr. Alexander, and Supplementary Statement Number 2," *The Accounting Review*, July 1955, pp. 383–399). Dein's rebuttal ("Price Level Adjustments: Rejoinder to Professor Husband," *The Accounting Review*, January 1956, pp. 58–63) emphasizes a requirement of specifying ways in which price-level-adjusted financial statements contribute to sound investment decisions. The reader may want to review these articles not so much for an orderly treatment of price-level-adjustment techniques as for the further experience of identifying assumptions that underlie particular accounting-treatment proposals. These articles also provide leads into literature that is relevant to the making of a critical appraisal of financial reporting practices and requirements, an area beyond the aim of the present course and syllabus.

The thread of continuity in the several Statements and in the Paton and Littleton monograph has been the underlying premise that historical costs (or acquisition price aggregates) should be allocated to periods during which associated economic resources are employed. Allocation to product is a secondary operation, controlled by more specific assumptions regarding categories of costs which can be deferred, modes of "flow" or "attachment" of costs to product, and persuasiveness of the more indirect formulas for association. Balance-sheet valuations are derived as residuals from the income-determination process. The so-called "matching" of costs and revenues is a process of deductive application of the rules of operation established as premises.

Some consideration has been given in the collateral literature of the field to the problem of choosing among alternative methods, say on depreciation, on the basis either of the "realism" of the fundamental premises or of expected consequences from their employment. For example, the appropriateness of declining-balance depreciation is deemed to depend on the pattern of "service-flow" from the asset. Or the choice between straight-line depreciation and varying-amount depreciation is associated with the objective of protecting investors from the machinations of management.

The following two chapters of this syllabus focus on an instance of the yearning for security and the search for its fulfillment through actions apparently based on the assumption of a unitary world. Those chapters deal with a phase of the activities of the Accounting Principles Board of the American Institute of Certified Public Accountants. That body was charged with the responsibility of "finding" the relatively small group of postulates which, it was believed, supported the structure of financial relations in the business world. It was assumed that the postulates, once identified, would constitute the building blocks with which a structure of accounting principles for guiding accounting determinations could be erected.

READINGS

PATON, W. A., AND A. C. LITTLETON, *An Introduction to Corporate Accounting Standards,* Chapters 1 and 2.

AMERICAN ACCOUNTING ASSOCIATION, Committee on Concepts and Standards Underlying Corporate Financial Statements, "Price Level Changes and Financial Statements," Supplementary Statement No. 2, *The Accounting Review,* October 1951, pp. 468-474.

HILL, THOMAS M., "An Analysis of Supplementary Statement No. 2," *The Accounting Review,* January 1952, pp. 16-24.

KOHLER, ERIC L., "Why Not Retain Historical Cost?" *Journal of Accountancy,* October 1963, pp. 35-41. Attention is directed especially to pp. 39-40 on "What today are the virtues inherent in historical cost?"

QUESTIONS

1. How do the Paton and Littleton tests for soundness of accounting standards compare with the requirements of the scientific method?

2. What do Paton and Littleton mean by the requirement of an "integrated conception"? Does the significant presentation of

financial information depend on its fitting a mold of "integrated conception"? Do Paton and Littleton place the same degree of emphasis as does Dewey on the requirement of controlled experimentation for the warrantability of assertions?

3. Assuming that a standards "tool" should be so designed as to compromise effectively the interests of managers, investors, and other primary groups, what criteria for compromise of group interests are suggested by Paton and Littleton other than "practical tool" and "legitimate needs"?

4. Does the Paton and Littleton requirement of "groundedness" negate the use of the experimental approach to knowledge and the use of the scientific method in accounting? Is "groundedness" only a partial requirement for accounting standards?

5. Is "business entity" better viewed as a concept which controls the choice of particular accounting-treatment rules or as expressing the identification of a problem area? Should particular variants of the enterprise concept be selected for their functional relations to the identified problem?

6. Should the significance of the entity concept be determined by the activities and relations of the firm or vice versa?

7. Can you state the basic Paton and Littleton proposition that is associated with the continuity of activity concept? In what senses has the term "going concern" been used in recent accounting literature?

8. In what manner is the Paton and Littleton proposition about earning power "strengthened" by the "concept of continuity"? Is the probability of the "truth" of a proposition increased by the fact that the general concept employed is used also in other propositions? Are the answers to these questions related to the Paton and Littleton requirement of "integrated conception"?

9. Can you explain accounting income in terms of a realization concept? Does the realization concept apply only to revenues as distinguished from net income? Does realization depend upon "objective" facts exclusive of estimates? Is the determination of realization based on assumptions about the relative stability of the external economy? Is the realization doctrine in accounting based on adoption of the going-concern point of view?

10. Is the concept of "embodied service potential" a fiction? If so, is it a useful fiction?

11. In what sense are costs "recaptured"? Which costs are recaptured? Does the term "recapture" explain any part of the

accounting process? Is "recapture" an operational term? Is the term used to identify a mathematical difference between aggregates?

12. Is the Paton and Littleton statement of a matching ideal more than an identification of a common problem situation? Does the statement suggest particular approaches to solutions? Does the statement indicate elements in qualitative situations that are relevant to solutions of the problem? Does the statement provide a basis for instituting and controlling operations for testing hypothetical solutions to the problem? Is the statement a scientific proposition?

13. How is the matching concept related to the notion of continuity of enterprise activity? Are different criteria of association appropriate where the attention is on the venture or project than where the problem encompasses varied activities occurring within a common time period? Are different matching tools suggested for the planning of integral activities than for the planning of changes in an existing complex of activities? Do most investment decisions fall in the former or the latter context?

14. Should criteria for associating effort *ex post* and accomplishment *ex post* be related to a purpose of testing the soundness of past decisions? What are some implications for appropriate association tools where past events are examined for their bearing on present decisions about potentials?

15. How is the matching concept related to the notion that costs attach? May a "belief" in "clinging costs" remove the problem of matching from the area of scientific inquiry?

16. What behavioral assumptions do you find in the Paton and Littleton exposition of accounting theory? Is their statement of accounting theory a complete hypothesis about consequences following from particular accounting choices as communicated. Do Paton and Littleton assume that accounting data as communicated provide only one ingredient in a mix; that decisions are made on a wide variety of considerations, and the reporting of so-called "accounting income" does not automatically (behaviorally) set off a series of consequences?

17. Can you restate the "concepts" of "measured consideration," "costs attach," and "effort and accomplishment" as a set of connected propositions constituting an element of the theory of conventional accounting?

18. In 1922 Paton said that any accounting "assumption, prin-

ciple, or procedure is . . . justified if it adequately serves the end in view . . ." (*Accounting Theory*, p. 472). Is the allocation-of-cost assumption of the function of accounting more fully justified if the end in view is taken to be the reporting to stockholders of the "margin by which their original equity is increased" (ibid., p. 497) than if the end in view is regarded as indicating to stockholders the change in the earning-power potential of the business?

19. When Hill, reflecting the viewpoint of the committee on Supplementary Statement No. 2, removed "historical nominal dollar method" from the protective shadow of tradition, was his emphasis on "historical" or on "nominal"? Was the allocation-of-cost function of accounting implicit in the recommendations of Supplementary Statement No. 2?

20. In what sense is the "earning process" of a firm an "experience"? What is the relation of conventional income accounting to that "experience"?

21. Were Hill and the committee on Supplementary Statement No. 2 correct in their statement that the use of replacement cost for valuation "necessarily" assumes that replacement will be made in kind? Should a distinction be made here between replacement cost and replacement requirements? Do you think that this consideration was basic to the committee's conclusion that price-level adjustments to historical cost data should be made and supplementarily reported?

22. Is the argument of the committee on Supplementary Statement No. 2, that purchasing-power adjustments to historical-cost data will make the latter "significantly nearer to true comparability," a deductive conclusion? An empirical finding? Should its acceptance rest on the criterion of "making sense"?

23. Does the conclusion that price-level adjustments will yield data which will be better than if no adjustment had been made necessarily follow from premises about the use and significance of historical-cost income data? May an attempted price-level adjustment in some cases offset the effect of individual market price changes?

24. Does Littleton's response to "the challenge of replacement prices" (*Structure of Accounting Theory*, pp. 222-230) involve an examination of consequences from the use of price-level-adjusted income figures? Can you express Littleton's general argument in syllogistic form? Can Littleton's argument be analogized to a prescription of conditions for entering a chain-link circle?

25. In the fall of 1964 a Study Group at the University of Illinois presented *A Statement of Basic Accounting Postulates and Principles,* in apparent response to the findings and conclusions of Accounting Research Studies No. 1 and No. 3 published by the American Institute of Certified Public Accountants. The latter documents will be analyzed in Chapters 8 and 9 of this syllabus. The Study Group's response adopted "the form of a recommended system of accounting postulates and principles" (Preface). In substance the Study Group's *Statement* is a reaffirmation and modernized elaboration of the assumption that "accounting is primarily a method of analysis based on a record of the exchange transactions . . . experienced by an enterprise . . ." (p. 1).

Equivalents of exchange transactions that could be admitted into the subject-area of "analytical-record" accounting data, as distinguished from "interpretation," were rigidly limited. The limitations were indicated both by the restrictedness of enumerated "equivalent economic events" (pp. 9, 15), and by specification of the criterion that includibility depends on a finding that the claimant event "produce results essentially the same as exchange transactions" (Postulate No. 3, p. 9).

Should the form in which propositions are communicated to readers be relied upon to characterize the related approach, as "postulational" or otherwise?

8

The Institute's "New Approach": The Postulates Foundation, and Accounting Research Study No. 1

The character of research effort emphasized by the American Institute of Certified Public Accountants shortly after 1959 was indicated in an earlier chapter of this syllabus. The official start of the new development in accounting research can be identified with President Jennings' appointment of a special study committee in December, 1957. That committee interpreted their function of research recommendation as requiring a break with the past. The introductory statement in the committee's report to the Council of the Institute applied the criterion of "new approach" to the organization and direction of research activities, and to the "promulgation" of, and "adherence" to, accounting principles.

A primary objective of the Institute, however, remained unchanged: the purpose of research effort was to identify and influence the content of "generally accepted accounting principles." And the influencing process was to be continually directed to a molding of practice within the limitation that "the areas of difference and inconsistency" should be "narrowed." There is a striking resemblance to the approach of Socrates who sought to support "traditional beliefs" with "rational investigation and proof" (Dewey, *Reconstruction of Philosophy*, p. 17).

The committee's conception of the new effort was orderly. On the basis of pervasive research activity, reference marks would be established at three levels. "Generally accepted accounting principles" would be determined largely by institutional (Accounting Principles Board of the Institute) acceptance of alternative "principles." The "principle" favored by the Accounting Principles Board was to be referrable, in support, to "a fairly broad set of coordinated accounting principles." (The commitee's report did not consider the possibility that a rejected, alternative "principle" might also derive support from the "broad set" of principles.) A condition for adoption of the particular "broad set" of principles was that the set be "based on" a set of "postulates." The committee's preconception of postulates limited their number to "a few," and asserted their function to be "the basic assumptions on which principles rest." Control of the selection of assumptions to serve as postulates was seen to be almost automatic and as yielding unde- batable conclusions: "They necessarily are derived from the eco- nomic and political environment and from the modes of thought and customs of all segments of the business community." The prin- cipal problem at this stage was to make the postulates explicit.

The conceived relationship of propositions (specific rules implementing broad principles and the latter resting on a few postulates) was to be reflected also in the ordering of the research effort. A research study on identification of postulates was to pro- vide direction to a research study on broad principles, and the Accounting Principles Board's reaction to the research study pro- posals on postulates and broad principles would provide the guide- lines for researchers in specific areas such as long-term leases and income tax allocation. The committee's report did not envisage the possibility that the process might break down.

The "new approach" had an auspicious beginning. The form and operations of the administrative structure were rationalized. Research projects were instituted in the basic areas of postulates and broad principles. Other research projects, in specific areas, were assigned to academic personnel.

In 1961 the research study on basic postulates was published (Accounting Research Study No. 1. *The Basic Postulates of Ac- counting*). The foreword appropriately absolved the Institute from any responsibility for the conclusions and recommendations. Only one member of the related Advisory Committee expressed an ex- ception to the findings of the author and Director of Accounting Research of the Institute. Leonard Spacek doubted that the basic propositions of the monograph were "postulates" in an operational sense of providing "a foundation for the formulation of accounting principles." More basically, Spacek disagreed with the "new ap- proach" adopted by the Council of the Institute; in Spacek's view progress in establishing accounting standards depends on a primary step of defining "the purposes and objectives" of accounting.

The companion research study on broad principles was published in 1962 (Accounting Research Study No. 3. *A Tentative Set of Broad Accounting Principles for Business Enterprises*). Emergence of this study from the horizon brought mixed reactions, of acclaim, of surprise and shock, or of wishes to reverse the course of events. The critical reaction, that of the Accounting Principles Board, was that ". . . these studies[joining the study on postulates to that on broad principles] are too radically different from present generally accepted accounting principles for acceptance at this time." (April 13, 1962, Statement by the Accounting Principles Board, accompanying the distribution of Accounting Research Study No. 3).

The original plan was for a statement of broad principles, to provide a frame of reference for specific rules of the order represented in the earlier Accounting Research Bulletins. The function of the latter had generally been regarded as contributing to the identification of "generally accepted accounting principles." Thus "broad principles" were to be differentiated from "generally accepted accounting principles." Yet the "broad principles" of Accounting Research Study No. 3 were rejected by the Accounting Principles Board on the ground of their deviation from "present generally accepted accounting principles." Was the research project faulty? Was the attention of the Study directed to rules instead of to principles? If the American Accounting Association-sponsored Statements provided the image could any other scope have been expected?

The Postulational Approach to Accounting Standards

Even though a meaning can be denoted by various symbols, and the terms "postulates," "principles," "axioms," and "assumptions" have sometimes been used interchangeably, it may be helpful to note that the term "postulate" in accounting is not a recent innovation. In Chapter 20 of his *Accounting Theory* (published in 1922, and reprinted in 1962 by A.S.P. Accounting Studies Press, Ltd.) Paton used the term "postulates of accounting" to identify what later came to be called "underlying concepts";

specifically mentioned were the concepts of "business entity," "going concern," stability of the monetary unit, the accrual or "attachment" of costs, the representative status of the balance sheet for indicating current financial condition, and the notion that assets are independent and equal summations. Paton clearly identified the meaning of postulate as an assumption on which operational procedures and interpretations of significance were based. The postulates were to be accepted tentatively, subject to being tested for their suitability as means to "the end in view." "Few if any" of the postulates "are capable of complete demonstration" (ibid., p. 472). George O. May is also frequently referred to when the question of the early use of the term "postulates" is raised.

Character and Function of Postulates in Study No. 1

What did the author of Accounting Research Study No. 1 expressly adopt as the general meaning within which he would elaborate categories of postulates? The author's introduction to the monograph indicated that he could find the direction for his study somewhere in the meanings in which the term "postulate" had been used in accounting literature. Rejecting the meaning used in Accounting Terminology Bulletin No. 1 and in *Changing Concepts of Business Income,* which coincided with what Paton and Littleton's monograph and the later Statements of the several committees of the American Accounting Association had called "underlying concepts," the author of Accounting Research Study No. 1 chose to use the term "postulate" in the sense for which he he found internal evidence in the instructions by which he was charged. Postulates underlie principles, and the latter provide a connecting link with guiding rules. Supporting this choice of meaning for the term "postulate" was his impression that "propositions of accounting theory and practice" could be readily classified with the aid of the selected meaning of the term "postulate." Was he, then, taking "principles" as given, rather than as propositions to be derived after appropriate "postulates" had been identified?

The author of the study puzzled over the selection of an "approach" to an unstated problem. Of course, he had noted a problem of selecting the sense in which the term "postulates" would be used. Was the problem implicitly the "finding" of elusive postulates to serve as a basis for principles? Or was the problem that of identifying the conditions for the warrantedness of propositions? Using short symbols, the "approaches" discarded were: the "axiomatic," the "ethical or sociological," and the so-called "pragmatic." The approach chosen was to move through the world of economics and politics (representing abstractions from the existential world) and to make mental observations of the interests that accountants exhibited in the abstracted economic and political data. The latter he called a "problem-oriented approach."

The axiomatic approach to knowledge which the author discarded is also called "the postulational" approach by other writers. The author strangely divided accounting into an "a priori part" and an "empirical part." The author of the study may be interpreted as saying that an axiomatic approach does not yield complete knowledge, that it must be paralleled by another approach which, by observation of particulars, is depended on for generalizations constituting a part of knowledge, and that in some unidentified way the results of the rationalist and empiricist approaches interact to yield a residue of "true" knowledge. But the author chose to pursue neither of these two avenues to knowledge, nor their combination. The axiomatic approach yields incomplete results. An empirical approach, though regarded as complementing the rationalist approach (identified here with the axiomatic approach), required "more pragmatic procedures," and apparently was not an appropriate method in social inquiry. Unfortunately, the author was sidetracked by adopting the narrow meaning of "pragmatic" as a synonym for "useful" (or "it will work"). Instead of pursuing an inquiry into interactions in economic affairs, and extending the study into means-consequences patterns, the author was stopped by the imagined sign: "Danger: do your professional commitments interfere with an unbiased analysis? Can you indicate possible means-consequences from a point of view without fostering a 'special interest'? The 'standpoint of society' mentioned in Accounting Research Bulletin 43, at page 7, may be a mirage."

The author of the study took note also of a currently competitive approach to the formulation of accounting principles which had been earlier stressed by DR Scott. The latter had pointed to fundamental conceptions of truth, justice, and fairness, whose content varies with time and place. Means-consequences determinations were implicit in this type of analysis, and judgments of acceptance were guided by the observed parallelism of those patterns with contemporary concepts of fairness or similar fundamental conception. Spacek was a current advocate of that point of view for the selection of accounting standards, and was a member of the Accounting Principles Board. It is likely that the writer of Accounting Research Study No. 1 would want to anticipate the dissent which would be based on relating accounting rules to the conception of fairness. That writer did mention and reject "an ethical or sociological approach" on the ground that the inherent subjectivity destroyed its usefulness to serve as a standard for accounting practice. The limitations of an ethical approach to the determination of accounting standards could be avoided, in his opinion, by adopting a "problem-oriented approach."

The "problem-oriented" approach is not identical with a problem approach to knowledge. The first stage in a scientific analysis is an identification of a problem, with at least a suggestion of the direction of solution of the problem. Selection of data to serve as facts is controlled by a conception of the operations to be performed with and upon the selected data so as to reach an end in view. The data are selected from what Dewey called the "matrix" of inquiry. The author of Accounting Research Study No. 1 also proceeded to draw some data from a matrix, although he used the term "environment." He needed a principle of selection. He did not, however, select data from the environment in correspondence with a conception of their suitability as means to an end in view; he did not employ a problem approach. Instead, the selection was to be controlled by some prior knowledge about "the *problems* that accountants deal with." More particularly, the "principle" of selection was to be the personal observation of, or possibly agreement on, some relationship between the datum and the accountants' occupational interests. The area of choice was indeed wide.

What, finally, was the approach that the author of Accounting Research Study No. 1 settled upon to characterize his inquiry? Having stated, in a roundabout manner, that he will focus on those "problems with which accountants concern themselves," he concludes that the most fruitful approach to the formulation of standards of practice places the emphasis on deductive reasoning. Presumably he regards deductive reasoning as the establishment of the implications of a set of propositions according to agreed-upon rules of operations performed upon the meanings adopted as entities in the meanings-system. Further, presumably only those implications having possible reference to the existential world would be selected for study.

In our opinion, the author thus returned to an acceptance of the axiomatic approach which he had expressly rejected, unless the reference to real-world possibilities distinguishes postulates from axioms. But he arrived at this position without indicating specific problems calling for solutions, or ends in view for which particular data would be more suitable means than would other data. He also did not propose a hypothesis to serve as a conceptual medium for the selection and ordering of data as facts in a manner that would yield other data to serve as partial tests of the hypothesis. In a negative vein, the author repudiated the efficacy of classifying objects by modes of interaction, for the reason that, in his opinion, interactions are unstable in the social world, where modes of behavior shift with the acquisition of knowledge about the immediately preceding patterns of conduct. Again in our opinion, the author began his task of setting out "postulates" without having presented his readers with a basis for judging whether he would have satisfied his "charge," or whether the propositions to be presented would help to establish warrantedness for subsequent statements on standards of accounting practice.

Interpretations of Accounting Research Study No. 1

How has Accounting Research Study No. 1 been interpreted? Some evidence of the operative meanings of the several postulates may be obtained from an examination of a succeeding monograph on accounting principles, since the planned pattern was that the postulates should serve as "a base for" broad principles of accounting. The relation of "postulates" to "broad principles" will be considered further in the next chapter of this syllabus. At this point we will examine some review literature on the postulates study, made prior to the publication of the principles portion of the study. Three major critical items are: Cannon, "Discussion Notes on 'The Basic Postulates of Accounting,'" (*Journal of Accountancy*, February 1962, pp. 42-53); a book review by Littleton (*The Accounting Review*, July 1962, pp. 602-605); and a reporting of comments received by invitation of the American Institute of Certified Public Accountants (*Journal of Accountancy*, January 1963, pp. 44-55). These items are briefly examined in the following paragraphs of this section.

Cannon's "Discussion Notes"

Cannon, an insurance company executive and a member of the Accounting Principles Board, strongly supported the approach and results of Accounting Research Study No. 1. His article on "Discussion Notes" referred to above was expressly motivated by a desire to extend discussion of the Study from the national convention of the Institute to grass-roots meetings of practicing accountants. While Cannon's article did contain a reprint of the 14 postulates and selected discussion from the study, and did present a synopsis of how postulates drawn from the study could be associated with three selected practical problems, the main burden of Cannon's participation in providing content for the article was to justify the postulational approach to accounting standards. The problem was to gain greater credence for financial statements through reducing the number of alternatives accepted for presenting data that were taken to be basically similar.

More fundamentally, according to Cannon, the problem was to provide management and investors with value data relevant to decision-making. The approaches followed by accountants could be adjudged as progressive improvements, but the tempo of improvement had slackened in a field where change was accelerating. An ideal solution had not been achieved through the ad hoc approach of the Accounting Procedure Committee or the attempt otherwise to identify "generally accepted accounting principles." Other influences were either insufficient (as the influence of the Securities and Exchange Commission on "fostering a healthy evolution"), or operated as deterrents (as the policies of regulatory commissions, and the influence of courts and of textbooks), or threatened to disrupt the orderly advance of the accounting profession (as the inroads of engineers and other competitors in offering management services).

Within the accounting profession specific proposals for institutional changes were receiving vigorous advocacy (as Spacek's proposal for an "Accounting Court"). The Institute's answer to the demands for constructive action had been the creation of an Accounting Principles Board and the adoption of a program of research for the development of accounting standards through a specific doctrine that a rational basis for accounting standards can be found in a chronological progression from postulates to broad principles to standards of practice.

In the concluding section of his article, Cannon specified postulates that were relevant to a solution of the price-level problem, and similarly for the accounting for long-term leases and for pension plans. The demonstration ended where it began; with the specification of postulates which the writer considered relevant. In each case an assertion was made that the writer's conclusion was determined by the "logical structure" represented by the associated postulates, presumably in the order in which they were cited.

In the final paragraph of the article Cannon characterized the postulates as both satisfying the Institute's "charge" to the researcher and as providing evidence that the original conception of the postulates—broad principles—standards progression was sound. Some reservation about their efficacy was indicated, however, by references to the postulates as "self-evident," as possessing the property of being "by no means innocuous," and by suggesting their function as helping to "clarify" thought "within" a meanings-system.

Littleton's book review

A major part of Littleton's review is concerned with speculations about the meanings of the postulates presented in Accounting Research Study No. 1, and about the relationships among the postulates and between the postulates and principles. He thought that the five "imperatives" of "continuity, objectivity, consistency, stable unit, disclosure," might "deal with goals"; yet they are all directed to the dominant goal of effective communication. Littleton would have chosen the descriptive term "persuasive concept" instead of "imperatives" for them. Taking the A, B, and C postulates together,

Littleton regarded them both as demonstrative and as descriptive: he pointed to some selected relationships and concluded that the relationships demonstrated "a unifying force within accounting"; and their aggregative import was "to describe the characteristics of accounting technology concisely and rather completely."

Littleton answered his own question of whether the C propositions were "presented as goals or standards to be achieved" in the affirmative, and drew the implication that the A and B postulates were in the relationship of means to the ends expressed by the C propositions.

The reviewer saw that some unsatisfactory conclusions followed from his interpretation of the intended relationships among the sets of postulates, and he suggested alternative interpretations for the A group of postulates. His ultimate evaluation was a combination of an optimistic attitude toward the cumulative effect of research studies and a recognition of the need for testing the stated postulates, along with principles to be associated with the postulates, by reference to consequences in terms of guides to accounting practice. In stating the latter pragmatic standard, Littleton himself criticized the author's narrow use of the term "pragmatism" as meaning "usefulness."

Invited comments

The Journal of Accountancy Staff analyzed 52 letters which had been received in response to an invitation for comments on Accounting Research Study No. 1. The letters cannot be regarded as representative of the populations of accountants or users of accounting information; the number is too small, and no information is presented which would indicate that the letters have the qualities of a sample. The comments do, however, suggest attitudes and points of view applied to the interpretation of the "basic postulates." They should be regarded as exemplary rather than as representative. The suggestion of the Journal Staff that the dearth of adverse critical comments indicates general agreement with the study's results has not been supported by subsequent developments.

The zenith of reactions may be stated as agreement both with the approach of the Study and with the postulates selected by its author. Acceptance was justified or determined in the minds of some readers by reference to a tautological attribute of "funda-mentalness," to an a priori standard of "self-evidence," or to ration-alist criteria of "soundly reasoned," "logical," "well-organized," or expressive of "clear thought." For some commentators the dove-tailing of propositions among the A, B, and C groups was accepted as substantiating each of the sets of propositions.

Other commentators accepted the method of approach used for Study No. 1 but were not satisfied with the aggregate of prop-ositions advanced as postulates. Mere "self-evidence" was a test of validity, but propositions could exhibit this quality without either being important enough for formal specification or providing a directive for the selection of other propositions that exhibited the relation of "principles" to the "postulates." In the extreme instance it could be denied that the postulates were capable of elucidation into "principles."

Another variant of generally favorable reaction questioned the number of postulates, on the basis that the specified 14 postu-lates was either too large or too small a number. A comprehensive list would have included a proposition on "communication," and another on "materiality."

The nadir of reactions was the denial that the approach used for Accounting Research Study No. 1 was appropriate for the de-velopment of rules of accounting treatment. In some cases the basis for this position was inchoate, or merely suggested by reference to a wish for a more "realistic" approach, or to the need for a demon-stration of the mode of connection between "postulates" and "prin-ciples." A predisposition toward a definitional approach to the identification of accounting principles seems to have been reflected both in queries about the meaning of the word "postulate" and in assertions that appropriate research should begin with the identifi-cation of the objectives of accounting. One aspect of the latter ap-proach is an overemphasis on inventorying those operations that can be called "accounting" and a corresponding de-emphasis on means-consequences relations in which "accounting" operations are one variety of means.

A very few comments (which may have been parts of even fewer individual letters) presented the problem approach as a positive alternative to the approach of the study. The problem approach used in the method of science has been presented earlier in this syllabus as starting with the recognition of an unsettled situation, and as involving the formulation of a problem in terms which also suggest a means of reaching an end in view, or modified qualitative situation. The means-pattern is refined into a hypothesis that provides the principle of selecting data to serve as means and which constitutes a guide for the development of other data which will serve to test the hypothesis. One commentator pointed out that the number or source of postulates should be regarded as an object of knowledge, or a termination of inquiry, and not as an a priori limitation on the scope or direction of inquiry. In similar vein is a comment which favored "the pragmatic approach of C. S. Peirce," but which saw a distinction between that approach and an "ethical approach."

In a general context ethical judgments are not inconsistent with the problem approach. In Dewey's view such judgments are applied to alternative sets of means-consequences patterns, and not solely to an end-in-view. For example, the development of a community of superior persons may be an attractive ideal, but the means-consequences pattern adopted to attain this goal during the Nazi regime in Germany generally evokes repulsion. As another example, the decision to limit atmospheric nuclear tests is based, not on judgments of their irrelevance for greater knowledge of the physical world, but in great part on an evaluation of the entire means-consequences pattern, including an evaluation of the consequences of employing atmospheric explosions as means.

The so-called "ethical approach" was also interpreted, in the study and in some comments, as exemplified by the Spacek proposal for limiting the content of postulates to "fairness." Others of the comments would have included "fairness" among a larger group of postulates. It may be, as one commentator suggested, that concentration on a single requirement of "fairness" would tend to move the inquiry from a jurisdictionally contained quest for the definition of those activities that constitute "accounting" to a problem approach directed toward identifying the conditions under which particular types of consequences may be anticipated. Under the latter approach the classification of modes of operation or types of data as "accounting," "economic," or "managerially significant" would be a secondary rather than a primary objective.

It may be assumed that those comments which criticized

particular postulates in isolation or in relation to others of the study's postulates were in general agreement with the approach adopted for the development of accounting principles. There is, of course, the possibility that disapproval of the entire body of postulates was presented discriminately rather than solely in the aggregate; for example, a statement that the Group A postulates lack functional effectiveness for the determination of broad accounting principles is not a warrant for regarding the Group B and Group C postulates as suitable for this purpose.

Some comments expressed uncertainty about the intended or proper relationship among the three groups of postulates. Possibly some of the A postulates should have been included in the C group, or a fourth group should have been established. Or the B postulates should have been presented more subordinately, as corollaries of the A postulates. Further, the C postulates could have been further subordinated under the interpretation that they constituted "working rules." We have seen that Littleton's book review on Accounting Research Study No. 1 suggested that the C group expressed accounting objectives, in relation to which the A and B postulates were means.

READINGS

JENNINGS, ALVIN R., "Present-Day Challenges in Financial Reporting," *Journal of Accountancy*, January 1958, pp. 28-34. Read especially the sections on "restrictions of existing research methods," and "new approach to research."

"Report to Council of the Special Committee on Research Program," *Journal of Accountancy*, December 1958, pp. 62-68.

POWELL, WELDON, "Report on the Accounting Research Activities of the American Institute of Certified Public Accountants," *The Accounting Review*, January 1961, pp. 26-31.

Accounting Research Study No. 1. *The Basic Postulates of Accounting*.

QUESTIONS

1. Assuming that the Powell report on accounting research activities included in the study assignments represents the thinking back of the "new approach" to research by the American Institute of Certified Public Accountants, did that approach follow the philosophy of Littleton? If the test of sound practice was a proper relationship among formulations of tentative principles, why was it necessary to begin with the disclosure of "postulates"?

2. If business actions are influenced by accounting reports, are any ethical problems raised by the profession's "experimentation with new ideas," which may lead to changed accounting-treatment rules? Would the ethical problems be different if only "sound" experimentation were practiced? Can the soundness be determined prior to the experiment? Is Jennings making a plea for the use of controlled experimentation in ascertaining the consequences of alternative accounting practices?

3. Jennings proposed in 1958 that a research organization for examining "basic accounting assumptions" should also "develop authoritative statements." How could the authoritative quality be attained if the research organization were not controlled by the Institute? If the signification is to "the authority of ideas," by what process do ideas attain the quality of authoritativeness? Was it Jennings' intention that statements of the research organization would *become* "authoritative" only if the Institute's governing body "accepted" the statement?

4. Did the prestige of the Institute suffer from the rejection, by the Accounting Principles Board, of accounting-principles recommendations that had been prepared and submitted by its own research agency? Was the relation of the research organization to the Institute merely a matter of "housekeeping arrangements"?

5. Was the charge to the Special Committee on Research Program consistent with President Jennings' outlook on principles development as "in the nature of pure research"? Does the committee's statement of its charge indicate any contemplated change in the process of official declaration and enforcement of rules identified as "principles"? Was the new research effort to be directed to finding more effective means for accomplishing the continuing objective? Was it contemplated that the force of administrative pronouncement would be supplanted by the inductive influence of ideas? Were intellectual restrictions in fact placed on the re-

searchers? Or should the research arrangement be regarded as contractual, with the researchers voluntarily accepting whatever limitations on research approach and effort were part of the contract offer?

6. Did the Special Committee on Research Program agree with Littleton's position that the formation of accounting principles was largely a process of formulation? Did it assume that the finally declared principles would be found within the present body of "generally accepted accounting principles"? What was meant by the phrase "to advance the written expression of" and by the term "what constitutes"?

7. Can you identify the "something more than a survey of existing practice" which was stated as a research requirement by the Special Committee on Research Program? What is the function of "postulates" in such a program?

8. Did the Report of the Special Committee on Research Program indicate that principles were to be directly and deductively related to postulates? Were any meanings clearly specified for the terms "derived from," "underlying," "foundation for," or "on the basis of"? Is the phrase "stem from" an improvement?

9. Was it "absurd" to expect that the "broad principles" to be reported by the researchers as a basis for accounting practice would be directly and deductively implicated in a small set of objectively existent postulates which could be found and identified by a competent scholar? (See the statement by Sprouse in "The 'Radically Different' Principles of Accounting Research Study No. 3," *Journal of Accountancy,* May 1964, p. 64.) Did the statement of the Special Committee on Research Program indicate that they contemplated such a process and relationship?

10. According to the Special Committee on Research Program, the expected specific research studies "would indicate logical solutions to accounting problems in relation to basic postulates and broad principles." What do you find to be the meaning of "logical" as used here? Does it mean deductively implicated? Since neither the proposed "basic postulates and broad principles" nor substitutes were accepted by the Accounting Principles Board, is the "logical" status of specific research studies indefinite?

11. If a set of "basic postulates and broad principles" had been adopted by the Accounting Principles Board, and if a specific research study were subsequently to develop all of the chief implications for the particular problem area under investigation,

would the statement of those implications be "authoritative" in any degree? What did the Special Committee on Research Report mean by the qualifier "not highly" in connection with authoritative?

12. What is your reaction to the statement, made by the author of Accounting Research Study No. 1, that there can be an "a priori part of accounting"? Did that author suggest that an "empirical part of accounting" could be "known" independently of "reason"? Can you relate his presuppositions to strains of philosophical thought suggested by the names Descartes and Kant? Do you think that his reference to "known by reason alone" is more to the traditional rationalism of Descartes or to a logical rationalism which emphasizes the drawing-out of implicated meanings by a deductive process? If the latter reference is intended, should the subject-matter be limited to mathematical (uninterpreted) systems?

13. Does the author's characterization of Accounting Research Study No. 1 as an "objective inquiry" suggest that the research problem is the finding of objectively existent postulates? (See statement by Sprouse in *Journal of Accountancy*, May 1964, p. 64 regarding objectively existent postulates.) Or that no value judgments are involved in the statement of postulates that will serve as a foundation for accounting principles? Would value judgment not be relevant because of the assumption that everyone's valuation is identical, that is, that the propositions expressing postulates are "self-evident"?

14. If accounting postulates are self-evident, why is "deductive reasoning" a necessary step in their determination? Is it because there are layers of postulates, and those that would be self-evident if identified: (a) are not generally in the consciousness of the ordinary person, and (b) the more basic or self-evident postulates ineluctably "lead to" only a specified set of more generalized statements, which may then loosely be called postulates? Were the 14 postulates of Accounting Research Study No. 1 deductively "derived from" an unspecified number of self-evident propositions? But if the inquiry is completely "objective," and no value judgments are involved in the determination of postulates, what is the import of the caution that the researcher should give "careful attention to what 'ought' to be the case"? If the postulates are self-evident but the selection of principles involves value judgments, is the relationship between postulates and principles merely implicatory? Is there an error in regarding postulates as self-evident?

15. The author of Accounting Research Study No. 1 associates Chambers with the use of the scientific method in accounting. The article cited as making "a strong case for" that method was not assigned for study. From your reading of Chambers, did you find a sustained attempt to use the scientific method? Did Chambers characteristically employ the postulational method? Are the two methods identical?

16. Which of Chambers' "propositions" (from his "Detail for a Blueprint" article) are most like Postulates A-1 and A-3 of Accounting Research Study No. 1? Is the subject of Postulate A-2 an implicit proposition for Chambers?

17. Do you find any significance in the fact that Postulates A-1 through A-4 indicate action or process whereas Postulate A-5 is in the Aristotelian subject-predicate form? Are the first four postulates more "behavioral"? Can you apply Dewey's distinction between "gross, macroscopic" data and "refined products of inquiry"? Littleton (book review of Accounting Research Study No. 1, *The Accounting Review*, July 1962, pp. 602-605) would have preferred a different formulation of Postulate A-5 such that "money-price" would be represented as "a quantitative experience to be stored in an account."

18. If, as suggested by the author of Accounting Research Study No. 1, other propositions contradictory to Postulates A-1 through A-5 could have been selected as possible postulates, what criterion was used to select the particular propositions represented as Postulates A-1 through A-5?

9

The Relation
of "Broad Principles" to the "Postulates,"
and Accounting Research Study No. 3

It has been said by the principal author of Accounting Research Study No. 3 that the unique propositions offered by that publication were (1) the use of net realizable value for inventories where such value could be "objectively determined" (and otherwise the use of replacement costs), and (2) the use of replacement costs for plant and equipment where their "objective measurement" criterion was met. Current acceptance of the principle of discounting future receivables and payables was referred to W. A. Paton's *Accounting Theory*, originally published in 1922, and to numerous subsequent "good" textbooks. (Sprouse, "The 'Radically Different' Principles of Accounting Research Study No. 3," *Journal of Accountancy*, May 1964, p. 66.)

The relative emphasis on value as against the "costs-attach" set of doctrines of more conventional accounting was thought by Vatter ("Postulates and Principles," *Journal of Accounting Research*, Vol. 1, No. 2, Autumn 1963, p. 196) to have been implied by Accounting Research Study No. 1. Littleton (book review on Accounting Research Study No. 3, *The Accounting Review*, January 1963, p. 221) selects as "the key section" the following statement from the Chapter 7 summary: "Section D . . . that 'the problem of measuring (pricing, valuing) an asset is the problem of measuring its future services . . .'" In our view the "future services" idea is secondary. The main point is the acceptance of the objective of identifying changes in "economic" value of assets and debts, and of interpreting those changes as resultants of certain interactivities generally designated as price-level changes, market forces, and managerial effort.

Relation of "Broad Principles" to the "Postulates"

Were these, as well as the other, "less radical" accounting-treatment rules of Accounting Research Study No. 3 derived by deduction from the 14 postulates of Accounting Research Study No. 1? Were the postulates "discovered" by appropriate observation of the environment, where the discovery implied "an objective existence and obvious validity" for the postulates? Were the postulates broad enough in meaning to permit the deductive derivation of other principles? Would observation of the environment reveal alternative postulates from which still other principles could be deductively derived?

The method of inquiry described by Dewey, and presented as the method of science, specifies sharply contrasting conditions for the warrantability of propositions. There a hypothesis is interpreted as postulating outcomes, and controlled experimentation is utilized for testing the warrantedness of the hypothesis. Also, in the development of a hypothesis, data are selected provisionally, on the basis of their assumed serviceability as means toward the attainment of an end in view. "Basic" statements are not "given" to inquiry, no matter how skilled the observer or how long the observation. Data are abstracted from an environing situation in accordance with a controlling conception of their means-characteristics in relation to the purpose, or posited new situation to be attained.

An alternative set of "postulates"

It may, however, be instructive to present an alternative "set" of postulates in the Accounting Research Study No. 1 sense, and to consider whether that set is likely to find acceptance as "self-evident" or "a priori." If the alternative set of postulates is not readily acceptable as "self-evident," consider whether it exhibits this quality less than do the 14 postulates of Accounting Research Study No. 1. If the alternative set of postulates is acceptable as "self-evident," has the psychological support for a "self-evident postulates approach" been weakened? Still another issue would be raised if the implications for accounting-treatment rules, of the two sets of postulates, were different.

The alternative set of postulates is presented below, in three groups, X, Y, and Z:

X-GROUP

Postulate X-1.   Qualitative Attributes.   Qualitative attributes are the characteristics of objects on which choices are made, that is, for making decisions about the selection or rejection of things so that the objects acquired are correctly related to needs and desires.

Postulate X-2.   Utility.   The essential activity on which exchange depends is the creation of utility, or the qualitative characteristics of goods which satisfy needs and desires.

Postulate X-3.   Cooperation.   The creation of utility depends on the cooperative efforts of individuals in modern society.

Postulate X-4.   Continuity.   Creation of utility is continuous and depends upon both historical antecedents and expectations.

Postulate X-5.   Expression of Demand and Supply Factors.   Although the values of goods are ultimately unique to individuals, actions by individuals in respect to economic goods result in the adoption of a common denominator of value and in the expression of demand and supply factors through ratios of exchangeability or price.

Y-GROUP

Postulate Y-1.   Accounting Identity.   The results of the accounting process are expressed in a set of financial statements which reflects the accounting identity that "assets" equal "equities."

Postulate Y-2.   Bases of Accounting Data.   Accounting data are based either on a conventional ordering of figures according to agreed operations rules, or are guided by expectations that changes in materials which are justifiable by future correspondence between goods-qualities and desires can be effected within the pecuniary expectations of the intermediary.

Postulate Y-3.   Beneficiaries.   The results of the accounting process are expressed for the benefit of a number of interested classes of individuals, and the orientation is often toward the class of residual stockholders.

Postulate Y-4.   Incomplete Time Reference.   Since the operations of utility creation are continuous, and have ties both to the past and to the future, the attempt to evaluate the effects of activities identified with a specified period of time must be incomplete.

Z-GROUP

Postulte Z-1.   Flexibility.   Patterns of activities can be modified to correspond with changing needs and objectives, within a more comprehensive control field.

Postulate Z-2.   Scientific Method.   Changes in materials and in relationships (which are justifiable ultimately by reference to the matching of qualities and desires) should be taken into account wherever decisions about operations are implicated. To the maximum extent possible, conditions associated with observed change should be specified, and emphasis should be placed on achieving a public character for observations.

Postulate Z-3.   Consistency.   Where data and operations are selected for their relevance as means to specified ends in view, the consequences of the observance of the conditions of successful inquiry should define the meaning of consistency.

Postulate Z-4.   Tentative Acceptance of Standardization for the Measurement Unit.   Ends in view can be attained more readily by employing some data as means and rejecting other data; in this context it may be efficient to assume that the effect of variations in the meaning of the common denominator of value can be approximated by certain specific adjustments.

Postulate Z-5.   Functional Character of Accounting Reports.   Accounting reports should be functionally related to the attainment of specified ends in view, and this requirement imposes the condition that the information presented is relevant and that the communications system is efficient.

Some elements of the "postulates" sets compared

The author of Accounting Research Study No. 1 asserted that decisions about ends-means in the context of an economic society involve judgments of "more-less," that *quantitative* data are helpful in the contextual decision process. The comparative Postulate X-1, presented above, asserts that *qualitative* attributes are more fundamental in determining choice. The latter proposition would tend to start the inquiry at the level of the "gross and macroscopic," while the term "quantitative" as used in Postulate A-1 is closer to "the refined products of reflection." (John Ratner's "Introduction" to *Intelligence in the Modern World* presents the foregoing contrast as an aspect of John Dewey's philosophy, p. 89.)

Postulate A-2 states that the characteristic mode of satisfying wants through economic goods is through an exchange process. The parallel Postulate X-2 emphasizes the need for investigations which would direct activity so that the characteristic of exchangeability would obtain for goods. It highlights the creation of utilities, in the sense that it focuses on the need to study persons' wants as well as the physical world with its technologies. The "supply and demand factors" seem to be more fundamental concepts than is the concept of price or relative exchangeability.

Postulate A-3 may be viewed as a description of an observed mode of conducting affairs, of carrying on activities, in a generalized formulation. And Postulate B-3 is a description of a smaller-scope phenomenon, that "the results of the accounting process are expressed in terms of specific units or entities." The comparative Postulate X-3 emphasizes the need to *explain* particular organizations of activity. It poses the problem of coordinating effort through motivations and benefit justifications, and makes no assumptions about "entities" independent of persons in association. It leaves the "entity concept" for independent investigation.

Evaluation of the "postulates"—
"broad principles" connection

The comparisons made above are illustrative, and not exhaustive. It should be clear that established connotations of words make particular formulations of propositions more or less suitable as references for other ideas which lead to action proposals. Furthermore, the formulation of "postulates" as starting propositions implies the recognition of an indeterminate situation and ends in view. Thus it would not be improper to select conceptual data (here "postulates") for their possible means-characteristics in organizing a hypothesis in terms either of historical cost or of economic values.

In fact, the process of inquiry necessarily involves the selection of ideas and existential materials in correspondence with a conception of their efficacy in reaching an end in view. The test of particular selections of data and operations lies in the evaluated consequences. The back-and-forth movement between conceptions and data is in contrast with an assumed single-direction progression from "postulates" to intelligent actions. Conceivably the emphasis in a particular investigation could be on the development of mathematical models for "impressment" upon the state of affairs, as was indicated in Chapter 4 of this syllabus. Thus it is not strange that, as stated in the preface of Accounting Research Study No. 3, the original draft of that study was prepared antecedently to any close integration of that study with the "findings of the postulates study."

What is regrettable is that the authors did not break away from the misconception about a single-direction progression that underlay the "new approach" of the American Institute of Certified Public Accountants. Their insistence that statements of "principles" were "based on" postulates, and that particular postulates "led to" principles is indicative of an acquiescence in the official form of the "new research program," which was inconsistent with the process of scientific inquiry and which in fact was not justified by the products of the research effort as these are represented in Accounting Research Study No. 3. A by-product of the authors' insistence on the specific postulates-basis for their recommendations is the exposure of the latter to blanket rejection on the charge that their dependence on the asserted postulates structure was not demonstrated (as in Kohler, "Why Not Retain Historical Cost?" *Journal of Accountancy,* October 1963, p. 36).

The authors of Accounting Research Study No. 3 stated that they were guided by a requirement of "compatibility" with the "basic postulates" of Accounting Research Study No. 1. Presumably this meant that the "broad principles" should not be logically inconsistent with implications deductively determined from the "postulates" (Queenan, "Postulates: Their Place in Accounting Research," *Journal of Accountancy,* August 1962, pp. 24-33).

A possible interpretation of the stated dependence on the

postulates of Study No. 1 for the purpose of the principles of Study No. 3 is that the postulates were subconsciously formulated so that *they* would be "compatible" with principles which were selected on other grounds than that they were deduced from postulates. If a person were convinced that market values are important data in making and evaluating decisions, a quest for a "foundation" proposition might rest at a statement such as Postulate A-1, which refers to the action of making decisions in the context of economic goods, and which makes the assumption that actors attempt to relate means and consequences (as the meaning of acting rationally). Vatter interpreted Accounting Research Study No. 1, and especially Postulate B-2, as slanted toward a value approach, and away from a cost approach to accounting-treatment rules ("Postulates and Principles," *Journal of Accounting Research,* Vol. 1, No. 2, Autumn 1962, p. 187).

Of course, each of the joint authors of Accounting Research Study No. 3 might have had a different view of the relation of the accounting-treatment rules of Study No. 3 to the "postulates" of Study No. 1. The author of the postulates study expressed great earnestness in an adherence to a postulates-broad principles approach to accounting-treatment rules. The same philosophical predisposition may be gleaned from certain later writings by the same author, as in an article titled "Why Do We Need 'Postulates' and 'Principles'?" (*Journal of Accountancy,* December 1963, pp. 42-46).

To the principal author of Accounting Research Study No. 3, however, a quality of absurdity surrounded either a certain set of "simple-minded assumptions" or the suggestion that this set of assumptions in fact guided the new research effort of the American Institute of Certified Public Accountants. That set of assumptions included the notion that principles were derivable from postulates which themselves had "an objective existence and obvious validity," and were "discoverable" by analogy to the Greek "spectator" theory (Sprouse, "The 'Radically Different' Principles of Accounting Research Study No. 3," *Journal of Accountancy,* May 1964, p. 64)

In our opinion the "broad principles" advanced in Accounting Research Study No. 3 must be evaluated on grounds other than their implicatory relationships to the 14 postulates of Accounting Research Study No. 1. This is the case not merely because the postulates may be interpreted or reformulated to carry implications for competing accounting-treatment rules. This position is taken because the postulates themselves are subject to the appropriate tests for warranted assertions.

Obstacles to Interpretation of Study No. 3

One major difficulty in interpreting Accounting Research Study No. 3 has already been indicated. This is the use of language which is patterned after the one-direction doctrine that knowledge proceeds from postulates to broad principles to other principles. That verbal dependence required the use of mediating propositions for bridging the gap (or chasm) between postulates and principles. A second obstacle to ready understanding of the authors' meanings is the character of their writing in the study.

Neither a lack of correspondence of principles with postulates nor the involved presentation of the broad-principles study can justify a summary rejection of the latter's proposed accounting-treatment rules from consideration by students of accounting. Those treatment rules should be considered on their merits in comparison with alternative rules of treatment. But that evaluation is the subject of another course of study. At this point illustrations of the two types of obstacles to ready comprehension of the message of Study No. 3 will be presented.

The authors' doctrinal position and comprehensibility

Certain introductory statements in Accounting Research Study No. 3 suggest the carry-over of the "problem-oriented" approach of Study No. 1. Introductory chapter 1 begins with "accounting" rather than with problems within which accounting may be relevant. The "problem-oriented" approach of Accounting Research Study No. 1 is reflected also in the assumption that the search was for principles that would determine the content and order of *accounting* financial statements. Other data required for solving the problems of decision-makers could be supplied supplementarily, outside the *accounting* financial statements.

The authors justified the use of supplementary schedules by "extension of the definition," where the original sanction was provided by a Statement on Auditing Procedure. A second type of support for their particular definition of what constitutes *accounting* statements is a referral to Postulate B-1: "the results of the accounting process are expressed in a set of fundamentally related financial statements which articulate with each other and rest upon the same underlying data." Yet the verb "are" suggests that the articulation referred to in the postulate is that which was presently observable in practice. While the authors are taking the abstraction "articulation" and assigning it a new and extended meaning, nevertheless their emphasis will be on the recognized *accounting* statements.

The doctrine of one-directional progression from postulates to broad principles to rules was utilized also in the authors' statement that "the functions of accounting" were reached by following a path that "led" from "the first five postulates." Presumably the term "led to" was intended to refer to a "disclosure" that there were *only* those meanings implied in Postulates A-1 through A-5 that constitute or are reducible to Postulates B-1 through B-4 or to the stated functions of accounting (even though Moonitz regarded "postulate" as having a "wider range of significance than 'principle,' " in "Why Do We Need 'Postulates' and 'Principles'?" *Journal of Accountancy,* December 1963, p. 43). But suppose that another postulate were substituted for, say, Postulate A-4?

Postulate X-4 from this syllabus presents the "self-evident" proposition that "creation of utility is continuous and depends both upon historical antecedents and on expectations." Would it follow from Postulate X-4 that a "function of accounting" is "to assign the changes in resources to specifiable periods of time" as stated by Postulate B-4? Yet the authors have not presented any reason for preferring Postulate A-4 over other postulates, including a proposition like Postulate X-4.

A companion Postulate (Y-4) to X-4 might read: "since the operations of utility creation are continuous, and have ties both to the past and to the future, the attempt to evaluate the effects of activities identified with a specified period of time must be incomplete." Would the latter statement "lead to" the authors' statement of "the functions of accounting," including the function "to assign the changes to specifiable periods of time"? Would the problem of "measuring" changes in resources appear more formidable under the alternative statement of the postulate and its companion Postulate Y-4?

The authors of Accounting Research Study No. 3 were evidently aware that some additional requirement would seem necessary to permit a movement from "postulates" to "principles." Their introduction of such a mediating element further clouded their writing. Their "transition" operation appeared to be entirely mental, as expressed by the terms "clear recognition," "formulation," and "bearing in mind." The authors then stated a proposition with the antecedent being *not* the 14 postulates or a part of them, but the transitional step identified as "to bear in mind the major point that profit is attributable to the whole process of business activity, not just to the moment of sale." Did the authors mean that the process of deductive analysis from postulates to principles revealed that one or more of the 14 postulates carried the meaning, which is set out as the transition proposition, that "profit is attributable to the whole process of business activity"; and that now all that is necessary is to carry the deductive (implicatory) process further by examining the intermediately derived proposition that "profit is attributable to the whole process . . ."? Certainly the idea of profit-attributable-to-entire-process is basic to the authors' "principle" that market events may be recognized prior to the time of sale. The question is, how did the authors "move" from one or more of the 14 postulates to the "entire-process" inter-postulate? If there was no deductive "movement" the reference to a postulates-principles progression was specious.

Further, assuming that the inter-postulate of "entire-process" has been stated or derived, should not the "principle" of market-change recognition be referred to as a further deduction? Yet the authors say that they are now going to state the "principles necessary to *implement*" [1] the inter-postulate.

Other obstacles to ready interpretation

The judgment that it is not easy to understand the meanings in Accounting Research Study No. 3 relates not to what the authors omitted (for example, the principal author orally expressed a recognition that a treatment of transition problems would have enhanced

---

[1] Italics added.

the acceptance of the study), but to the way in which words and phrases are used. For example, the authors observe that knowledge progresses by moving from the general to the particular. Furthermore, Accounting Research Study No. 3 would restrict its effort "to make clear the implications of the principles . . ." (Preface, p. x). Apparently technical operations were not important; nor were the operations of technicians a source of knowledge in the classic Greek culture. In the view of the authors, the "principles" would determine the character of the "detailed rules." The authors do not look to the identification of specific changes under controlled conditions to yield the conclusions which, as conclusions, would *constitute* the principle of the case, where the case consists of specifically identified interactivities.

The main doctrine in Accounting Research Study No. 3 is that net income is the "measure" of "change in" assets and debts, and that the total change can be segmented in respect to "causal agents" of managerial effort, market forces, and price-level changes. The authors cast aside the "realization doctrine" as: (a) not being a "principle"; (b) not being "an essential feature of accounting because the concept lacks analytical precision"; and (c) as involving a choice with the "postulate of continuity" (going concern), to the disadvantage of the "realization" concept. The remainder of the study is primarily a quest for *measurement* standards and interpretation of value change.

Unfortunately, the authors do not continue their attention to assets and claims, but refer to "profit" as a "function," and the need to measure "changes." Designating "profit" as a function submerges the events whose meanings define profit. And abstractions such as "change" are not measurable; measurement processes should be applied to something else (say, particular assets) during a time span or at successive points in time. In a modern industrial complex, for example, jointly operating elements produce a *single* changed state of affairs as a consequence, and the association of component objects or events with types of "causal" factors involves complicated inferences. In any but the simplest situation of proportionality of input and output the association of portions of the total effect with a specific element is a matter of interpretation (Thomas, "Discounted Services Again: The Homogeneity Problem," *The Accounting Review*, January 1962, pp. 1-11). It is important that the assumptions underlying the inferences be disclosed, and this requirement is more likely to be honored where the attention is focused on things-changing than on specific rules that represent a proposal for defining change.

The authors of Accounting Research Study No. 3 did begin their consideration of "change" by directing attention to "measurements in the area of assets and liabilities," and they referred specifically to "changes in the assets and liabilities." But they soon shifted the discussion to inferences about the influence on value of identified or assumed events, called "transactions." When they write of the classification of changes they mean the selection and interpretation of events or assumptions about events in terms of their influence on value change. The authors' reference to Postulate B-2 for an identification of "kinds of changes" is in the same pattern. Nor does their specification of classes of influence meet the problem. Although price movements of specific goods may be identified by reference to market quotations, the classification of a price change by mode of influence rests on *theories* that discriminate between purchasing-power effects and market effects on the specific prices.

The joint authors write of a problem of "measuring" the "other changes." They are asking either: (a) how a change in the value of an asset aggregate, like an enterprise, can be assigned to particular components within the asset aggregate; (b) how an identified or assumed change in the value of a particular asset can measurably be associated with elements in an interactive complex which includes elements outside the control of the enterprise management; or (c) on what criteria an identified or assumed (inferred) event can be deemed to have measurable effects on the value of particular asset aggregates, or even on specific portions of the asset aggregate.

Their "answer" avoids the questions. They point to an accounting fact: the use of a "wide range" of valuation techniques. They leave the problem with the following statement: "The use of this wide range of measures is definitely in accord with the function of accounting and should be integrated into its principles." The authors apparently expect their readers to accept the suggestion that the "measurement" problem has been solved through the present employment of varied valuation techniques for different classes of assets (and variously for different enterprises), by making a psychological association with Postulate C-2 and the accountants' traditional attitude toward "objectivity." They say, "The 'imperative' requires objective measurement."

Can we conclude that there *is* objective measurement in the process by which accounting income is calculated? The authors point to the present fact that "accounting . . . already uses a wide range of measures." Do the authors ignore the problem of defining "measurement," and of explaining why the accountants' practice does involve the use of "measures" rather than arbitrary rules of thumb? How are the "measures" related to "measurement"? Is a "measure" the *result* of comparing successive correspondences of the thing measured with a standard? And does it involve specification of the conditions under which the measure of change was observed? Are the authors arguing that many measurement *standards* should be used, without specifying the meanings of the standards? Is "change" *defined* in terms of correspondence with specified standards under conditions where *the* meaning of the standard can be maintained? Should the "use of this wide range of measures" be "integrated into its principles"? Or should the "principles" be used to test the consistency of particular measurement rules? Are "principles" and "measurement rules" interconnected?

Philosophical and technical problems of measurement are receiving increasing attention in the accounting literature. The following articles illustrate that tendency: Bierman, Harold, J., "Measurement and Accounting," *The Accounting Review*, July 1963, pp. 501-507; Chambers, R. J., "Measurement and Objectivity in Accounting," *The Accounting Review*, April 1964, pp. 264-274; Anton, Hector R., "Some Aspects of Measurement and Accounting," *Journal of Accounting Research*, Vol. 2, No. 1, Spring 1964, pp. 1-9.

The foregoing comments are intended to illustrate difficulties in interpreting Accounting Research Study No. 3 even apart from an independent technical evaluation of the proposed accounting-treatment rules. The latter task is the responsibility of another accounting course.

Some indication of the present direction of research effort of the American Institute of Certified Public Accountants is included in the following chapter.

READINGS

VATTER, WILLIAM J., "Postulates and Principles," *Journal of Accounting Research*, Vol. 1, No. 2. Autumn 1963, pp. 188-197.
Accounting Research Study No. 3. *A Tentative Set of Broad Accounting Principles for Business Enterprises*, Chapters 1-4, and 7. Scan comments by members of advisory committees.
AICPA STAFF, "Comments on 'A Tentative Set of Broad Accounting Principles for Business Enterprises,'" *Journal of Accountancy*, April 1963, pp. 36-48.

QUESTIONS

1. The two Accounting Research Studies, No. 1 and No. 3, agree on a statement of the "functions of accounting." Are you able to show to the satisfaction of your listeners how Postulates A-1 and A-5 "lead to" the stated "functions of accounting"?

2. One stated function of accounting is "to assign the changes to specifiable periods of time." Can changes be assigned to periods, or is the time reference automatically determined in measurements "before" and "after"? Is the term "assign" used with the intention of relating a change to an antecedent condition, as a "cause" of the change? Have the authors adequately differentiated objective occurrences or events, such as a sale, a collection of cash, and so forth, from interpretation in reference to some theory of income determination? "Assignment" to a period seems to belong to the latter problem.

3. The author of Accounting Research Study No. 1 said that a "theory of valuation" was "covered in a general way" in that study. And he suggested that the condition for an integrated postulates-broad principles structure was a more specific coverage, in later publications, of the same ideas that constituted the postulates of Study No. 1. Did he then regard the forthcoming principles to be published as Accounting Research Study No. 3 to be deductively implicated in the statement of postulates?

4. Can you interpret the following statement from Cannon, "Discussion Notes on 'The Basic Postulates of Accounting'" (*Journal of Accountancy*, February 1962, pp. 42-53): "The determination of accounting 'principles' is almost always done backwards, by analogy, from the particular to the general . . . This is barely half of a scientific method"? Did the authors of Accounting Research Study No. 3 use a "forward" movement to accounting principles? Did they use "barely half of a scientific method"? Or is the notion of a single-direction movement inappropriate for describing the phase aspect of inquiry with its back-and-forth surges of data and controlling conceptions?

5. In the article cited above, Cannon characterized the postulates as "the beginning step in what we hope will be a logical development through a set of broad principles and finally to some specific rules." Do you think that this progression constituted the "forward" movement which Cannon contrasted with the typical "backward" movement, and which he might call the generous half of the scientific method (the complement of the "bare" half)? Does the indicated progression constitute moving "from the general to the particular"?

6. Is "cost" an operational concept under the view expressed by Cannon that ". . . we have . . . expanded the concept of cost to include any 'objective' measurement . . ."?

7. One comment on Accounting Research Study No. 1 reported by the Journal of Accountancy Staff (*Journal of Accountancy*, January 1963, pp. 44-55) stressed the importance of directing accounting research "toward scientific methods of research." In your opinion, does this criticism constitute an approval or disapproval of Study No. 1?

8. One commentator on Accounting Research Study No. 3 (*Journal of Accountancy*, April 1963, p. 36) related the "acceptability" of the Authors' recommendations to implications of their deviation from "today's generally accepted principles." Yet the Special Committee on Research Report had envisaged the results of Accounting Research Study No. 3 as intermediate between postulates and propositions that were or could become generally accepted as principles. In which category do the recommendations of the Study No. 3 best fit?

9. Thirty percent of the 42 letters received by the Research Division of the American Institute of Certified Public Accountants in response to the Institute's invitation to comment on Accounting Research Study No. 3 aligned their views with the previously expressed views of some of the members of the project advisory committees on the related Studies. As reported in the "Comments" article (*Journal of Accountancy*, April 1963, p. 37), only one of the committee-member comments appended to Accounting Re-

search Study No. 3 was not "generally critical of the conclusions reached in the study." The names of Blough and Werntz were included in each of the "typical" letters which described their views by this reference method.

The Werntz comment appended to Study No. 3 was directed largely to specific recommendations made by the Study, and the recommendations were criticized both on practical grounds and as departures from present, and presumably more desirable, reliance on cost allocations instead of market valuations. And in terms of communication quality, the study in its present form was found to present an inadequate differentiation of recommendations from existing practices.

The Blough comment elaborated the familiar doctrine of evolutionary development of accounting practices, and combined this reference standard for practices with a coherence test for those propositions which were formulations of present practices. Little provision was made for the process aspect of evolution, and the function of an accounting principles board was, by inference, interpreted as narrowing the areas of difference in the use of accounting-treatment rules by the method of eliminating some of the present practices without introducing other practices. In addition, the identification of a "principle" was closely associated with official actions of the Institute body, and relevant references were made to experienced problems in using appraisal data in the 1920s.

Neither of the comments was directed to an examination of the postulates of Study No. 1 or to any "logical" dependence of the authors' recommendations to the published postulates.

What additional criteria do you consider relevant for an evaluation of the recommendations of Accounting Research Study No. 3?

10. Evaluate each of the following statements from the collected comments (*Journal of Accountancy*, April 1963, p. 39) for its consistency with the scientific method: (a) "The principles proposed in this research study may be reasonable and perhaps quite logical from a purely theoretical point of view"; (b) "Accounting is a pragmatic art which has evolved through experience. It rests upon generally accepted accounting principles which, having been thus derived, represent primarily a distillation of the best in existing practice"; (c) ". . . in the evolutionary process of accounting principles and practice, many of the proposals may well prove worthy of adoption . . . Much proof and logic needs

to be offered as to their acceptability . . ." Would the publication of data prepared on the recommended basis through supplementary schedules constitute a sufficient "testing" of the new principles of data-treatment?

11. May the criticism that the recommendations of Accounting Research Study No. 3 are "too radically different for acceptance at this time" reflect a practical judgment independent of judgments about the desirability of consequences that would flow if the recommendations were in fact in use? Was this idea expressed in the Werntz comment on the need for a statement of "ground rules for a transition"?

12. Should the adoption of particular accounting-treatment rules for financial reporting be influenced by the consequence that the treatment rule under consideration is different from a present rule that coincides with an allowable income tax method?

13. Which of the recommendations of Accounting Research Study No. 3 do you regard as "basic departures from presently accepted principles"?

14. One comment on Accounting Research Study No. 3 (*Journal of Accountancy*, April 1963, p. 43) criticized that study for "recognizing profit upon completion of production activity rather than at point of sale." Did Study No. 3 make such a recommendation? (See also a comment by Sprouse in *Journal of Accountancy*, May 1964, p. 65, and his identification of the recommendations that were different from existing practice, at p. 66.)

15. What premises underlie the comment (*Journal of Accountancy*, April 1963, p. 43) that adoption and use of the valuation bases recommended by Accounting Research Study No. 3 "would negate two basic premises of present-day accounting theory"? (The latter premises were identified as lower-of-cost-or-market valuation for assets and the point-of-sale, income-realization standard.)

16. Would the use of replacement cost for pricing inventoriable assets and calculating cost of goods sold require its application "on a continuous basis" as contrasted with end-of-period adjustments?

17. Did commentators criticize the use of replacement cost for inventory items on the ground that: (a) replacement market quotations were not available; (b) practical difficulties of obtaining quotations were insurmountable or made the goal not worth the candle; (c) replacement market prices even under present lower-

of-cost-or-market practice are not significant; or (d) the extended use of replacement cost pricing as contemplated by the recommendations would influence quoted prices so as to make them no longer significant, or at least that even uninfluenced replacement-market prices are not significant for the "large blocks" of inventory that would be involved if the recommended pricing principle were generally used? If the criticisms rested on some conception of significance of replacement market prices, did the criticisms include a corollary proposition that pricing at inferred acquisition prices did give significant results? Did the criticisms rest on the premise that the balance sheet should not be used to show "values"?

18. Evaluate the comment (*Journal of Accountancy*, April 1963, p. 44) that "the authors of this research study have moved from a going-concern concept based on historical costs, objectively verifiable, to one based on economic values which are subjective."

19. One comment (*Journal of Accountancy*, April 1963, p. 48) seems to tie in the recommendations of Study No. 3 with a specific research process and with the postulates of Study No. 1. Do you read that comment to say that the recommendations stand or fall with the acceptance of the postulates-broad principles, single-direction process that was stated in the report of the Special Committee on Research Report and elaborated in the two research studies; and that the recommendations are not logically persuasive products of the postulates-principles process; therefore the recommended treatment rules are not supportable on other grounds?

20. How much of what Sprouse referred to in the context of "simple-minded assumption" ("The 'Radically Different' Principles of Accounting Research Study No. 3," *Journal of Accountancy*, May 1964, p. 62) must be met in order that the characterization will apply? Does the characterization apply severally, in the sense that simple-mindedness is additive? Is it simple-minded to assert that postulates "exist"? Did Vatter assert that postulates exist but that the authors of Research Studies No. 1 and No. 3 had identified the wrong thing under the name "postulates"? (*Journal of Accounting Research*, Vol. 1, No. 2, Autumn 1963, pp. 188-197.)

21. In what sense did Vatter choose to use the word "postulate" in his article on "Postulates and Principles" (*Journal of Accounting Research*, Vol. 1, No. 2, Autumn 1963, pp. 188-197)? What aspect of inquiry did Vatter identify with the word "postulate"? Was his emphasis on postulated outcomes under specified conditions or on postulated conditions that are necessary for the

explanation of observed events? If a word or other symbol has a tool function in inquiry, may the term "postulate" be used or discarded as desired, subject to practical conditions of intercommunication?

22. Can the notion of "objectivity" be put in propositional form so as to constitute a postulated condition that may be deemed necessary for the explanation of observed events? Did the author of Accounting Research Study No. 1 weaken his case by applying the term "imperative" to the notion of objectivity and expressing it in a "should be" form? Can "objectivity" be a postulated means, or would the alternative expression, in which an action or process is assigned the meaning of being objective, be more suitable? Under the latter approach would attention tend to be channeled away from questions of "the meaning of objectivity" to the assertibility of particular means-consequences relations? In the phrase "measurement *is* objectivity" (Vatter, *Journal of Accounting Research,* Vol. 1, No. 2, Autumn 1963, p. 190) has an action or process been equated to an abstract universal (nonexistential) term?

23. Expand the following statement from the assigned reading in Vatter's article (p. 194): ". . . postulates fill the gaps between what we do and what we cannot know."

24. Evaluate the following statement from Vatter's article (p. 194): Postulates "may be useful even when we know they are false." Can you relate this notion to Vaihinger's "as if," and to the accounting doctrine of "costs attach"?

25. What is your reaction to the following statement from Vatter's article (p. 196): "Principles . . . cannot be generated from hypotheses via deductive reasoning if they are to fit the problems of the world." Would this limitation, if valid, rule out the "interpreted mathematical systems" approach? Does Vatter confuse the testing of hypotheses through controlled experimentation with the process of constructing hypotheses? Or is his emphasis merely on the tentativeness of a deductively determined hypothesis prior to the verification that only its reference to experience (controlled observation) can give?

10

Summary
of Preceding Chapters and a Projection
of the Institute's Basic Research

Chapters 1, 2, and 3 of this syllabus were historical in form, although analytical in purpose. In addition to providing leads for a more intensive historical development of accounting thought, these chapters introduced ideas that were found to be currently in vogue in discussions on accounting-treatment rules. The idea of evolutionary development with or without an assumption that the unfolding is "in good hands" is currently used to justify existing practices. Change in basic economic and social conditions is currently referred to in connection with suggestions that accounting-treatment rules presently in use be modified. Specified conditions which were historically associated with the adoption of certain asset-valuation practices are contrasted with modern industrial and social conditions. Current problems have roots in the past.

An important function of Chapter 3 was the identification of a problem that the accounting profession faced as early as the 1930s and whose solution is still being sought. This problem is variously phrased. The official statement of the problem is that of "narrowing the areas of difference and inconsistency" in financial reporting practices. Accounting Research Study No. 1 termed it a problem of finding those basic postulates from which *the* principles of accounting could be derived. A practical aspect of the problem is the satisfying of public-reporting demands prior to the reflection of those demands in authoritative action by the Securities and Exchange Commission.

Accounting Theory and the Process of Inquiry

Beginning with Chapter 5 of this syllabus, an examination was made of certain accounting literature which assumed the formulation of a general accounting theory to be a goal. A number of writers examined the problem from the point of view of necessary conditions, that is, of requirements that would need to be met if an accounting theory were to result. Chapter 4 outlined Dewey's exposition of the requirements of successful inquiry as a standard for the requirements expressed by the accounting writers. This standard was termed the scientific method. Aspects of the scientific method were compared with those persuasive aspects of various other theories of knowledge or epistemologies, which may account for the influence of the latter on contemporary thought.

Littleton may be interpreted as pointing to the development of an accounting theory through a proper selection of generalizations about accounting practice. The correctness of the selection would be indicated by personal judgments about the degree of "interrelatedness" and unification of the collected propositions.

Chambers has been referred to as a strong proponent of the application of the scientific method to accounting (Accounting Research Study No. 1, p. 7). Yet Chambers' "Blueprint" article concentrated on only one phase of the operations by which propositions acquire assertibility. It was Chambers' principal contention that conclusions acceptable for directing accounting practice could be derived deductively by squeezing a comparatively few assumptions and/or axioms for their implications. Subsequently, in *Towards a General Theory of Accounting* (The Australian Society of Accountants Annual Lecture, 1961), Chambers extended his axiomatic or postulational approach in pursuance of the stated objective "to deduce from the nature of the environment of accounting the characteristics of a system which will serve the purposes for which it was or is designed." In this variety of deductive analysis the resulting system is constrained by a presumptive correspondence between the assumptions and the real world. In a more limited view, Chambers has made a valuable start toward the identification of assumptions that are implicated in positions on practice which accountants have adopted. (Chambers, *The Resolution of Some Paradoxes in Accounting*, liberally and effectively illustrates the "approach" that moves from practices to assumptions, in the sense outlined by Chambers in an article, "Why Bother with Postulates?" contained in the *Journal of Accounting Research*, Vol. 1, No. 1, Spring 1963, pp. 3-15.)

Devine's article on "Research Methodology and Accounting Theory Formation" lauded the "power" of mathematics in developing implications and disclosing necessary relationships among meanings. Initially the requirement of realism was to be subordinated to that of rigor. Subsequently, however, the mathematical systems were to be "interpreted" by introducing those meanings for variables which seemed to correspond to real-world patterns of affairs.

Bedford and Dopuch thought there must be more inter-play of deductive analysis with the selection and treatment of existential materials. They took issue with Devine's suggestion for first "squeezing out" and subsequently restoring the "purposive aspects" of the problem situation. The joint authors emphasized means-consequences considerations in accounting inquiry, and noted that the concept of means in relation to ends-in-view necessarily implies the appropriate combination of measured amounts of objects that constitute means. Their position accords with that of Dewey's *Logic* in respect to the requirement for evaluation of the entire means-consequence pattern developed as a possible mode of problem solution. "Welfare and ethical" considerations are not limited to the conceived final result. And Devine's proposal for "adding back" the normative considerations did not seem workable.

Particular Theory Formulations or Approaches

The writers noted above set out some specifications for the formulation of an accounting theory but did not undertake to develop any particular theory. In Chapter 6 attention was directed to recommendations of committees of the American Accounting Association on, first, a pattern of standards for accounting practice and, later, the concepts that should be used in formulating standards of practice. The 1936 Statement was expressly stated as depending in large part on adoption of the assumption that accounting should be regarded as allocating costs to periods and to product. The Paton and Littleton monograph, examined in Chapter 7 of this syllabus, was represented as stating the "theory" underlying the 1936 Statement.

The Paton and Littleton monograph is essentially an elaboration of the doctrine that accounting is a process of cost allocation. The rationale for that position relied upon selected associations of treatment rules with interpretations of concepts designated as "business entity," "continuity of activity," "measured consideration," "costs attach," "effort and accomplishment," and "verifiable, objective evidence." Some of the associations made by the authors were tenuous and not logically necessary (that is, the cost doctrine did not follow by necessary implication from the propositions representing the stated concepts).

Later Statements in the American Accounting Association series adhered to the historical-cost doctrine, except for a provision in the 1957 Statement with regard to the pricing of inventories. Statement No. 2 supplementing the 1948 Statement recommended exploration into price-level adjustments, and the 1957 Statement included price-level adjusted reports as necessary. But in both Statements the latter type of report was special, and outside the main stream of historical-cost reports.

Prior to 1959, organs of the American Institute of Certified Public Accountants approached accounting problems piecemeal. Published opinions of the Accounting Procedure Committee were represented as a major component of an open-ended set of "generally accepted accounting principles." Beginning in 1959 the Institute embarked on a novel project that might be compared to the voyage of Columbus. The end-in-view was only vaguely identified, and the termination was far different than had been regarded as a possibility at the time the voyage began. Yet the voyage had consequences independent of the ends sought by the sponsors. Also, the results of the Accounting Research Studies can be evaluated apart from the motivations of the Council of the Institute in adopting the new research program.

Accounting Research Study No. 1 and Accounting Research Study No. 3 were examined in Chapters 8 and 9 of this syllabus. The postulational approach of Study No. 1 is quite similar to that of Chambers, especially in the latter's 1961 publication on *Towards a General Theory of Accounting,* but also in Chambers' "Blueprint" article. The Study No. 1 postulates were complex propositions, and the author's coalescence of ideas in only 14 propositions may have been influenced by the charter assumption that the relevant postulates were "few in number." Probably the most significant of the several selected postulates were A-2 and B-2, which specified an exchange economy and referred valuations to prices associated with "present, or future exchanges" as a possibility. The collection of "broad principles" presented in Accounting Research Study No. 3 emphasized valuation over cost allocation, and developed propositions which were consistent with that interpretation of the accountants' objective (except possibly in the area of depreciation accounting).

A Possible Return to the "Observation of Experience"

Before 1959 accounting spokesmen frequently explained practices, and particularly choices among accounting-treatment rules for financial reporting, as resting ultimately on "experienced judgment." Verbal justification of the practices might be a desirable embellishment for a profession, especially since it was not necessary. Or at least it was not necessary prior to certain popular demands for more information about the rationale of accounting practices. A statement of the "foundations" of accounting practices might even help the profession by "showing up" false practices, which would evidently be those practices that did not fit into the tight deductive arrangement of ideas which the attempt at rationalization must reveal.

Littleton's views on accounting-theory formulation, even where they were not fully understood, were often relied upon to support existing practices. Sometimes the accounting writer restated Littleton's early thesis of a predetermined destiny for accounting, toward which all developments were tending. In this use, the ultimate explanation for any practice was that it was part of a slow evolutionary development. On this premise, an almost insurmountable burden was placed on the proponent of any accounting-treatment rule that was not currently represented in practice. Yet there were diverse practices in seemingly similar situations. It seemed necessary to discriminate between good and bad practices, and that operation required reference to some framework of theory.

Littleton may justly be regarded as the apologist of accounting practice. According to his own account he started with practice, observing closely and formulating propositions that related particular practices as means to discerned purposes. Now it was necessary to distinguish the good practices from the bad practices. Littleton's ultimate reference seemed to be a particular set of propositions which for Littleton had the personal psychological support of a conclusion that this set of propositions met a metaphysical test of constituting a "part" of an (unknowable) "whole." The set of propositions was "true" because the individual propositions "cohered."

Here, then, was the reference framework to which propositions expressing possible accounting principles (propositions that associated particular practices as means with discerned purposes) were to be related. Only those practices which, when formulated as "principles," maintained the coherence quality of the principles set were "good" practices. Littleton provided a theory framework which not merely justified existing practices generally. It provided a rationalization of that set of practices which has elliptically been referred to as expressing the historical-cost doctrine. Littleton verbalized a personal, individual reference standard around which those persons who were sympathetic toward the historical-cost standard could rally.

The motivations that lay behind the "new approach" of the American Institute of Certified Public Accountants in 1959 will probably never be fully described. Increased public criticism of variations in accounting-treatment rules had been noted. A desire to examine the evidence completely and without prejudice is evident in individual writings. It is unfortunate that the mode of investigation and the expectations of findings were prescribed by the governing body of professional accountants. Apart from the question of the suitability of the accounting-treatment rules proposed by Accounting Research Study No. 3 for corporate financial reporting, the doctrinal setting in which those recommendations were presented is analogous to the well-known "two strikes against the batter."

The April, 1962, reaction of the Accounting Principles Board has already been indicated. The proposed postulates and principles were rejected. The stated justification for the Board action was that the postulates and principles were "too radically different." The "principles" proposed in Accounting Research Study No. 3 were "different," but the postulational approach was formally in accord with the official charge to the researchers. The explanation of the Board's action may lie more in motivations and predispositions than in polemics.

The Accounting Principles Board is currently issuing "opinions" on limited topics of current interest. This activity does not constitute a significant change from the issuance of bulletins by the Accounting Procedure Committee prior to 1960. There appears to be a greater breadth of exposure of pronouncements prior to their official adoption, and more paragraphs are devoted to discussion than was typical for the Bulletin statements. But the selections have been largely ad hoc, and the argument references are varied and incomplete.

The next significant event in the "new" program of the Institute may be the publication of a study on the codification of "generally accepted accounting principles." This project was put into operation by the second Director of Accounting Research of the Institute. Publication of the latter Study is to be made by a later Director of Accounting Research, and the character and import of that study cannot be stated with definiteness at this time. Its definite characterization as part of a "new approach" to research by the Institute must await its publication.

Twenty-five years before the rejection of Accounting Research Studies No. 1 and No. 3 a kind of inventory of accounting "principles" had been taken by Sanders, Hatfield, and Moore, and the results published as *A Statement of Accounting Principles.* In June, 1963, the Accounting Principles Board approved a project that would again involve a fundamental reference to "experience." Practices were to be observed, and principles "identified." Codification of principles was part of the research project which was to be implemented by the new Director of Accounting Research.

Some indication of the possible character of the forthcoming report on the inventorying and codification of accounting principles may be gleaned from earlier publications by the research director on this general subject. In addition to a May, 1962, article

("Quest for Accounting Principles," *Journal of Accountancy*, May 1962, pp. 45-50), which is identical with the comments of Paul Grady published as a supplement to Accounting Research Study No. 3, an "Outline for Inventory of Generally Accepted Accounting Principles for Business Enterprises" was published in November, 1963 (*Journal of Accountancy*, pp. 52-55). The content of the two articles is generally the same except that the latter article blocks out a tentative outline in which the principal content of the earlier article is reproduced as Part VI, and the earlier article contains a longer introductory statement.

In the introductory portion of the earlier article Grady characterizes the proper approach to the statement of accounting principles as one of identification as contrasted with discovery. Attention should be limited to existing practices; possible practices that are not now "generally" used will have no place in the contemplated inventory or in the codification. The process of stating accounting principles should be logically and chronologically separated into two stages; inventorying is the initial step, to be followed by the development of "a useful pattern of arrangement or classification." The facts are there, in the accounting environment.

Has the Accounting Principles Board made public a long-range research program or a philosophy of accounting research? How can the "new approach" to accounting research be currently characterized? Will future research projects of a fundamental nature reflect the interests and beliefs of the incumbent Director of Accounting Research? Will the research approach of the future aim at "integration of practical and conceptual approaches," where the products of the latter are typified by the Accounting Research Bulletins of the American Institute of Accountants and the periodic Statements sponsored by the American Accounting Association, respectively? (See Storey, *The Search for Accounting Principles*, p. 64, for this independent judgment of a proper approach, by the person who became the Institute's third Director of Accounting Research.)

READINGS

GRADY, PAUL, "Outline for Inventory of Generally Accepted Accounting Principles for Business Enterprises," *Journal of Ac-*

countancy, November 1963, pp. 52-55. See also comments of
Paul Grady, published as a supplement to Accounting Research Study No. 3.

STOREY, REED K., "Accounting Principles: AAA and AICPA," *Journal of Accountancy,* June 1964, pp. 47-55.

QUESTIONS

1. Which of the following meanings of "accounting principle" may be found in the literature? (a) A force inherent in
Nature which is instrumental in effecting a predetermined design
or destiny for accounting; (b) a rule of operation which is sufficiently general that a number of areas of application have been
recognized; (c) a rule of operation which is associated with either
widespread use or formal approval by a quasi-governmental or
professional body; (d) that formulation of an objective and a
means which constitutes an integral part of a coherence system;
(e) an accounting procedure; and (f) an element of a recognized
accounting theory.

2. Littleton's book review on Accounting Research Study No.
1 (*The Accounting Review,* July 1962, pp. 602-605) leaned toward the interpretation of the C postulates as goals or objectives.
In a symposium article, "Is Further Uniformity Desirable or Possible?" (*Journal of Accountancy,* April 1961, pp. 35-41), Peloubet
identified "basic principles" by enumeration: adequacy of disclosure, conservatism, materiality, conventional descriptiveness, and
the only "new" principle, residuality of the balance sheet. What
similarity is there between Peloubet's "basic principles" and the
C postulates including the Accounting Research Study No. 1 discussion on materiality and conservatism?

3. In what sense is the term "principle" used in the auditors'
opinion: "in accordance with generally accepted accounting principles . . ."? Could the word "acceptable" be substituted for "accepted" without necessitating any change in the profession's policy
on unqualified certificates?

4. Are accounting statements in published financial reports
of corporations presently designed for study by investment analysts,
for reading by "the man in the street," or are they otherwise
oriented?

5. Have you observed any indications of a "Gresham's law"

of alternative accounting principles? May the spread of one of a number of alternative accounting principles and the disappearance of the alternates be interpreted as "the survival of the fittest"? Is the latter concept employed in an exposition of biologic evolution?

6. Can reliance be placed on "evolutionary development" for unifying the structure of accounting principles? If so, what is the function of professional accountants in the evolutionary process? What influences act upon professional accountants for the carrying-out of that function? Can professional accountants "alter" the course of evolutionary development? If deliberative and action processes of professional accountants can determine the content of accounting principles, what modification, if any, is necessary in your meaning of "evolutionary development"?

7. If it is the plan of the Grady research project (named by reference to the published article in which the project was outlined) to "separate the 'shells' of" principles "from the 'sands' of" unacceptable practices, what is the character and pattern of the screen which will be used? Do you regard LIFO inventory pricing as an application of the historical-cost principle in its Income Statement aspect?

8. In your opinion is the admonition of the Grady outline (*Journal of Accountancy*, November 1963, pp. 52-55), "to account . . . in such manner as to fairly present . . ." a member of the body of "generally accepted accounting principles"? Were the recommendations of Accounting Research Study No. 3 intended to promote "fair presentation"?

9. Is it your expectation that the project for inventorying and codifying accounting principles will use the criterion of professional agreement for determining the content of the proposed inventory? Is agreement on the present content of generally accepted accounting principles likely to provide a criterion for settling other, current, problems of accounting treatment? Is the latter function to be assigned to the projected codified version of the principles?

10. Can you explain how "the scrub brush of good accrual accounting" can be used to solve problems such as those of income tax allocation, treatment of the investment credit, or long-term leases? (The quotation is from Grady, "Outline for Inventory of Generally Accepted Accounting Principles for Business Enterprises," *Journal of Accountancy*, November 1963, pp. 52-55.)

11. In what sense does Storey use the term "practical" in his observation that "the conceptual and the practical approaches to accounting principles seem to be complementary . . ."? In what sense does he use the term "practice" in his advocacy of "the union of concept and practice"? ("Accounting Principles: AAA and AICPA," *Journal of Accountancy*, June 1964, pp. 54, 55.) May the term "practice" be used to refer to existential materials in inquiry, suggested by "conceptual" materials of the "if-then" type?

12. Williams and Griffin (*The Mathematical Dimension of Accountancy*, p. 2) view "theory and practice," in the sense of "abstract formulations and specific applications," as 'inextricably interrelated." If "concept" in the Storey sense can be deliberately withheld from "union" with "practice," how does that meaning of "concept" differ from the Williams and Griffin meaning of "theory"?

11

Other Lines
of Accounting Thought

In this chapter an opportunity will be given to examine other recommendations for the determination of standards of practice for
public financial reporting. We have already noted the argument
that present accounting practice is a result of a slow evolutionary
development. The implication for the present and the future may
be that no positive action in shaping standards is required; the
presumption may be that each business will use those practices
which provide the greatest benefit to it, and that the body of practices will be molded in correspondence with changing environmental conditions and changing needs. That point of view has not
been acceptable to the Securities and Exchange Commission. The
present official position of the American Institute of Certified Public Accountants is that the number of variations in practice, either
absolutely or relative to an apparently similar situation, should be
reduced. Introduction of the factor of human purpose and organized action provides the basis for deliberative consideration of any
and all of the practices in use.

A Proposal Analogous to Establishment
of Legal Precedent

An example of the participation of purposive human conduct
in an "evolutionary" development is presented by the conception
of "the common law." Within the system of English jurisprudence,
"principles" of right conduct have been established and modified
on a case-by-case basis in correspondence with a controlling conception that similar cases should receive similar treatment. Assigned readings in this chapter of the syllabus show the use of the
common-law analogy in recommendations about the determination of accounting standards. In Spacek's proposal, the "Account-

ing Court" is not a fully public judicial body, but is a part of the machinery of "self-regulation" by the profession.

In a more recent article ("A Suggested Solution to the Principles Dilemma," *The Accounting Review,* April 1964, pp. 275-284) Spacek centered his proposal on current action by the Accounting Principles Board to declare what constituted proper and authoritative treatment-rules. Defense of their soundness through a demonstration of the underlying reasoning was to be deferred because of the urgent need for immediate professional action. Declared principles might be subsequently modified as it appeared that the supporting reasoning was "erroneous." No proposal for an Accounting Court was made in the latter article.

Spacek's comment appended to Accounting Research Study No. 3 is evidence of his disagreement with the postulational approach authorized by the Council of the Institute and implemented by the publication of Accounting Research Study No. 1. The notion that there should be a single foundation postulate, "fairness," is elaborated in an Arthur Andersen booklet, *The Postulate of Accounting.* Our interpretation is that the Spacek disagreement with the approach of Accounting Research Study No. 1 is more basic than is represented by the assertion that Spacek substituted one postulate, that of "fairness," for multipostulates. Spacek's chief reliance for the achievement of justice through a deliberative determination of accounting standards was on the mechanism of full critical argument by all interested persons. By analogy, criticism of the bases of court judgments, published in Law Review articles and in textbooks, has been an influential factor in maintaining the stature of the professed principle of *stare decisis* in the law.

A weakness of the "precedent" approach to the formulation of directive propositions is that cases tend to be decided on the basis of apparent or even superficial similarities in the patterns of data constituting the subject-matter for the inquiry. Classifications are likely to be made on the basis of immediate associations rather than probable consequences. Another limitation on the method of drawing conclusions on the basis of an "on all fours" doctrine, which is the ideal situation for the application of precedent, is that accounting determinations involve abstractions in high degree, and are made in an environment of complex physical and business arrangements. If, however, rules were to be expressed as functions of identified economic and political conditions that take expected consequences into account, then the deliberative, argumentative case-by-case approach governed by the objective of providing similar treatment in similar situations would seem to have merit where the determinative mechanism is democratically responsive.

In the April, 1964, article by Spacek referred to above, the writer contained his suggestions within a more limited scope. Action was to be taken by the Accounting Principles Board's determination of proper procedures without waiting for a broad social deliberative process. The urgent problem was that of reaching an authoritative position *within* the accounting profession.

The Institute Council's action on authority of the Accounting Principles Board should be read in connection with the latter's Opinion No. 2. For a reference to a public debate on the proposal that accountants be required to direct attention to "departures from" majority positions of the Accounting Principles Board, see an editorial on pages 33 and 34 of the March, 1964, *Journal of Accountancy*. A modified proposal was approved by the Institute's executive committee (*Journal of Accountancy*, April 1964, p. 9).

Principles by Agreement

If the problem is correctly stated as one of noncomparability of financial reports among firms because of the use of different statistical-treatment rules, would not the problem be solved if every firm used the same treatment rule in the "same situation"? Although this might be the long-run tendency under the doctrine of precedent applied by an Accounting Court, could not the process be speeded up by agreement of the listed corporations to use a common rule for an identified set of circumstances? The accounting profession would not "pronounce" one treatment rule to be required as the standard for receiving an unqualified "certificate," but would function as the leader in effecting agreement by the corporate clientele.

A proposal for the making of industry-by-industry agreements along these lines was contained in an article by a certified public accountant who was also vice-chairman of the Accounting Principles Board (Witschey, "The Business Need for Better Accounting Principles," *Journal of Accountancy*, January 1964, pp. 27-31). It was not clear from the cited article whether the author's positive proposal in fact used "principle" in the sense in which that word was defined by him in a subsequent paragraph: ". . . the development of criteria which will indicate the appropriate way to treat an account in the particular circumstances." May the quoted statement be interpreted as emphasizing the very basic problem of identifying those "similar circumstances" for which a particular statistical treatment of data is appropriate?

The current problem of reaching "agreement" *within* the accounting profession was indicated in the preceding section. There the profession's function was regarded not as that of leadership in effecting agreement among segments of the public but of declaring rules reached under a representative principle as the standard for actions of the entire membership of the profession.

The Image of Management Accounting

It is sometimes asserted that the same concepts that are suitable for management use in the control and application of resources are suitable in the development of information for, say, stockholder use. And it is possible that the notions of budgeting, opportunity cost, or probability analysis, for example, could be utilized in presenting accounting analyses for stockholders whose major interests in corporations entail investment or disinvestment.

The important questions are (a) whether management-accounting processes are directed toward helping management to make numerous marginal decisions, where the decisions take into account differential consequences, and (b) whether the account summaries developed primarily for the purpose of facilitating that kind of decision about the kinds of resource controls within the corporation can be said to provide the kind of information most useful to stockholders. Edwards and Bell (*Theory and Measurement of Business Income*) do state that it is likely that the same "set of . . . principles" that is useful for business management is also useful for reporting to stockholders, and then turn to a proposal for management-accounting which analyzes business profit much as was done later in Accounting Research Study No. 3.

Where the emphasis is on accounting for management purposes, one may expect that forthcoming textbooks will rely increasingly on interpreted mathematical systems (or "models") and on statistical treatment of quantitative data. Attempts have been made to develop equilibrium models for the firm, in terms of account relationships and suggested external variables (Mattessich, "Mathematical Models in Business Accounting," *The Accounting Review,* July 1958, pp. 472-481) and as a development of microeconomic theory (see Boulding, *Reconstruction of Economics*). Other developments include linear programming and techniques of simulation.

A recent book by Mattessich (*Accounting and Analytical Methods*) has been characterized by the publisher as an attempt "to present a general theory of accounting . . ." which treats valuation "in the light of modern decision theory." Handy and Kurtz (*A Current Appraisal of the Behavioral Sciences,* Section 7, p. 126) point to the important contrast between decision theory in the sense of "the development of mathematical models," and decision theory in the older sense of applying standard techniques of social science inquiry to the problem of making choices among alternatives. While the mathematical emphasis on accounting-theory formulation should be studied for a recognition of its possible values for financial reporting standards, the caution should be observed that statistical decision theory as a component of the behavioral sciences is still in the early hypothesis stage. Mathematical models have already become an accepted mechanism in the areas of macroeconomics and national income analysis.

Unifying Research Efforts in Correspondence with the Requirements of Inquiry

The concern of the present syllabus has been with accounting thought from the viewpoint of corporate financial reporting. The standard of reference throughout the syllabus has been the requirements of scientific inquiry, especially as that method has been exposited by John Dewey. With the aid of that reference standard certain methods which have been advocated in the literature as approaches to accounting-theory formulation have been seen to be only phases of a more complete process of inquiry, and other assertions have been found to be incorrect statements of any phase of that process. Association of the latter type of statement with ideologies or strains of philosophical thought that were reasonably supposed to have had general influence on our culture helped to explain the notions which were divergent from the pattern of inquiry.

The unification of research effort has both negative and positive requirements. On the negative side, it would be necessary to correct the thinking that separates "theory" from "practice," and which sets the "academic" over against the "practical." Further, the notion of a one "true" accounting income as an ideal would be removed if the modern scientific outlook were to be adopted as the standard for accounting research. Both of the views just stated have become entrenched in the thinking of many accountants for whom there is one accounting philosophy *par excellence*. In addition, it would be necessary to overcome a tendency to justify present practices on the ground that they *are* the practices, or on metaphysical grounds of predetermined evolutionary development. In passing it may be noted that if writers intend no more by the term "evolution" than "change," it would constitute more efficient communication if they would use the word "change."

On the positive side, attainment of the posited unity of accounting research would entail the study of the method of science more closely for its potentialities in the field of human behavior. And accounting thought would be developed in the context of behavioral inquiry. The problem approach would regard accounting techniques as means in relation to ends in view. Performance of the "service function," which is said to be the goal of accountants, would require ascertaining the needs and purposes of those classes of persons for whom the services are performed. The means-characteristics of various financial reporting techniques and processes would need to be closely analyzed for their relationships to the specified goals of identified classes of users of accounting information. A corollary of this development would be the replacement of the "general purpose" concept of accounting statements.

There seem to be at least three major alternatives to the issuance of "general purpose" accounting statements. The one that seems to express most closely the adoption of the problem approach is for firms to publish, subject to the opinions of professional accountants, interpretive statements which are expressly associated with particular points of view that are attributed to identified classes of economic actors. Difficulties in specifying uses within the class of investors are pointed up by a member of the committee on the 1957 Statement of corporate accounting standards sponsored by the American Accounting Association (Vatter, "Another Look at the 1957 Statement," *The Accounting Review*, October 1962, p. 661).

A second alternative is the maintenance of the present format for the Balance Sheet and the Income Statement but with additional disclosure requirements. The latter could include an express disclaimer that the Balance Sheet is intended to portray values or that the net income figure meets generally accepted tests of statistical validity. The report could include positive statements of the premises on which the statements were constructed, as an extension of the recommendation made by the May committee in 1932.

Only the first of the two foregoing alternatives can be said to furnish the readers of the statements with deliberately relevant data. The relevance requirement might also be met without the publication of progress and status reports adapted to the problems and points of view of particular classes of interested persons. This could be accomplished through the issuance of schedules and exhibits that contain types and treatment of data thought to have some close connection with, say, the investment and disinvestment decisions of stockholders, but on a more factual and less interpretive plane. This type of reporting would not include a statement of assets and liabilities that shows *totals* in the manner of the present conventional Balance Sheet. Nor would it present any figure represented as "net income" or other crystallized indicator of relative progress for the firm. This third alternative may not be acceptable to a profession that has accepted the office of steward of the net income concept.

In our opinion the materials constituting this syllabus indicate the need for intelligent aggressive action by members of the accounting profession toward understanding community and business needs, and in establishing an appropriate functional relationship between accounting process and those needs. In its educational aspect, such action involves the adoption of a much broader viewpoint than in the past about the domain of an accounting curriculum. Interdisciplinary considerations are becoming increasingly important in the determination and solution of business problems. The "attest" function and the quality of independence can be sustained only on a demonstration that the conclusions and opinions of the accountant are *relevant*.

READINGS

SPACEK, LEONARD, "The Need for an Accounting Court," *The Accounting Review*, July 1958, pp. 368-379.

SPACEK, LEONARD, "A Suggested Solution to the Principles Dilemma," *The Accounting Review*, April 1964, pp. 275-284.

"American Institute Council Acts on Recommendation for Disclosure of Departures from APB Opinions; text of conclusions and recommendations of the Special Committee on Opinions of the APB as amended and adopted by the Institute's Council." *The Journal of Accountancy*, November 1964, p. 12.

GORDON, MYRON J., "Postulates, Principles and Research in Accounting," *The Accounting Review*, April 1964, pp. 251-263.

Letter by Robert E. Witschey in response to article by Robert N. Anthony on "Showdown on Accounting Principles," reprinted in *Journal of Accountancy*, November 1963, pp. 68-69.

BAXTER, W. T., "Recommendations on Accounting Theory," in *Studies in Accounting Theory*, ed. W. T. Baxter and Sidney Davidson, pp. 414-427.

QUESTIONS

1. Does Spacek argue that only one specific accounting-treatment rule can be demonstrated to be "fair" for a particular "situation"? In other words, will the "reasoning" involved in the showing of fairness demonstrate that one treatment is absolutely fair, and that all other proposed treatments must be rejected as absolutely unfair?

2. Under Spacek's proposal, is experimentation an element in the demonstration of fairness? Can the status of warranted assertibility be attained through the process of "analysis of the under-

lying reasoning"? Do you agree with Spacek ("Are Accounting Principles Generally Accepted?" *Journal of Accountancy,* April 1961, pp. 41-46) that the suggestion of experimentation in the selection of accounting principles is an "indication of lack of integrity"?

3. Does the identification of a particular accounting procedure as a component of the body of "generally accepted accounting principles" absolve the individual practitioner from responsibility for finding that the particular accounting procedure used is appropriate in the circumstances? If not, should the form of the auditors' opinion be modified to include an express statement that the procedures used were regarded by the accountant as appropriate in the circumstances of the particular company?

4. Does Spacek argue that the "fairness" of particular accounting-treatment rules, viewed as means, is judged by the "fairness" of the results following from the use of the several means in the concrete circumstances of the case? Does his argument involve the assumption that the consequences of the use of alternative accounting-treatment rules are not debatable, that is, that they can be known independent of experimentation?

5. May Spacek's argument be interpreted as based on a teleological assumption of an ultimate design for the universe and an ordering of parts so that the ideal "whole" will be most closely approximated? In what other sense can it be effectively argued that only one of alternative treatments can be demonstrated to be fair to the exclusion of all other treatments, and that the conclusion of "fairness" applies to all involved (interested) persons? Or that there is only one "net income" figure that "meets the needs of all segments of our society"?

6. Is Spacek arguing that professional accountants should recognize a requirement for evaluating the demands and needs of different social groups, and should work for the adoption of that accounting-means which will best *balance* the conflicting viewpoints? Or, restated, that an Accounting Court may be expected to effect the adoption of those accounting-treatment rules that will, in the continuing judgment of all groups in society, represent their agreement on the fairest combination of wealth creation and income distribution in society? Is Spacek's proposal basically a plea for accounting principles through (social) agreement? And is "fairness" a conclusion rather than a criterion?

7. In Spacek's proposal, how would issues come before the Accounting Court for determination? To what degree could the

national organization of professional accountants maintain the *status quo* of accounting principles by controlling the docket of the Accounting Court?

8. Arthur Andersen & Co. has made some public distribution of a pamphlet, *The Postulate of Accounting—What It Is, How It Is Determined, How It Should Be Used* (September 1960, Subject File AC 320, Item 2). On pages 37-43 there is an illustration of the manner in which the fairness postulate would be involved in the determination that a particular proposed treatment had the status or quality of a principle (or acceptable accounting-treatment rule). It appears that the demonstration involves the use of the syllogism.

The major premise of the syllogism appears to be: All obligations should be reflected in the Balance Sheet. The minor premise, then, is: Long-term lease is an obligation. From these two premises it follows that a long-term lease should be reflected in the Balance Sheet.

Can you evaluate the foregoing argument to the extent that its force depends on the syllogistic "demonstration"? What considerations are appropriate in deciding that all obligations should be reflected in the Balance Sheet? Could that determination be made by finding a universal meaning for "obligation," independent of an evaluation of the consequences following from the varied reporting of classes of information which could be comprehended within the category of "obligation"? Would the evaluation of consequences following from the varied reporting of long-term leases be a part of the more comprehensive study of the reporting of "obligations," and thus a component of a generalization that could be formally represented as a major premise of a syllogism? In other words, would long-term lease exemplify the kind of obligation involved in the establishment of the "principle" or hypothesis?

9. Did Gordon ("Postulates, Principles and Research in Accounting," *The Accounting Review*, April 1964, pp. 251-263) make the "simple-minded assumption" referred to in the article by Sprouse ("The 'Radically Different' Principles of Accounting Research Study No. 3," *Journal of Accountancy*, May 1964, p. 64)? Did the new research effort of the Institute proceed "in accordance with this view of the matter"? Were principles of accounting expected to be deductively derived from postulates?

10. Gordon indicated that the statement constituting, say, Postulate B-2 was "true" in the same sense that the statement "all men are mortal" is "true." Did Gordon confuse existential and

universal propositions, or regard the distinction as unimportant? Is the statement "All men are mortal" true in the sense that the meaning assigned to "mortality" is ascribed by definition to all organisms including man? Would the existential proposition more parallel to Postulate B-2 be that men, along with many other classes of objects, exhibit a maturation process which terminates in the loss of identity as an organized entity? Is the latter statement "no less relevant for the choice among alternative bases of valuation . . ." in the Gordon sense? In what sense is the word "relevant" used here?

11. In what sense does Gordon use the word "principle"? In the sense of a rule of accounting treatment that has broad (inclusive) meanings? Is any means-consequence evaluation involved in determining that a rule of accounting treatment constitutes a principle? Is there implicit the notion that the accounting-treatment rule must be at least a possible means for attaining an end in view? Did Gordon intend to include the recommendations of Accounting Research Study No. 3 within the scope of meaning of his term "principles"? If, say, inventories are valued generally at current cost, may the "accounting principle" be stated merely as the current cost rule of valuation? Or does the (tentative) statement of a principle involve a hypothesis about the consequences of using current-cost valuation?

12. Does Gordon say that his C-type postulates enter into the determination of whether a rule of accounting treatment constitutes a principle of accounting, or that they enter into a "choice" between alternative rules of accounting treatment both of which constitute principles of accounting? If Gordon uses the term "principle" in the sense of a generalized statement of data treatment, on the assumption that the data are "given," and if his C-type postulates are intended as devices to promote choices among principles in the sense stated in this sentence, in what way does independence of the accountant facilitate the choice? Is a means-consequence relation implicit in Gordon's analysis? Is the required independence of the accountant a condition for the effective association of accounting-treatment rules as means with identified ends in view other than special interests of the researcher?

13. Continuing with the issues raised by the preceding question, in what way does the generality of a statement of an accounting-treatment rule facilitate a choice among such rules? Would a choice between a historical-cost valuation rule and a current-cost valuation rule be promoted if the alternative rules

were stated in even more general terms? Does Gordon's expression of the necessity for "frequent change" refer to a scientific problem of adequately representing observed interactions or correlations? Or does it refer to the scientific problem of presenting a universal (nonexistential) relationship abstractly enough so that it may be compared with observations in many areas or circumstances? Or does it refer to the policy question of pronouncement that a particular rule shall represent a standard of treatment or a mandatory treatment rule?

14. How does the "objective of providing information" promote a choice among accounting-treatment rules? Is this an explicit statement of an implicit notion in Gordon's analysis that rules are selected on the basis of their expected means-function in attaining specified ends in view?

15. How does common sense definition of subject matters promote a choice between accounting-treatment rules? Is the issue merely one of effective communication? If so, is the label "truth"-postulate appropriate?

16. Ignoring Gordon's statement that his list of C-type postulates is not exhaustive, and looking only at the five which he selected to represent "criteria for choice," may his list be narrowed to one? On the assumption that inquiry is objective, impartial, scientifically oriented, is the sole "criterion for choice" represented by the necessary implication that the "objective of providing information" involves the association of accounting-treatment rules as means to specified ends in view? Is the "disclosure postulate" an integral element in the selection of a particular accounting-treatment rule? If so, is it incorrect to say that the disclosure postulate "comes into play only after" some other process has been relied upon to "establish" accounting-treatment rules?

17. Is Gordon's exposition of the significance of C-type postulates necessary in order to reach a conclusion that the accounting-treatment rules recommended by Accounting Reasearch Study No. 3 cannot be derived by necessary implication from the 14 postulates of Accounting Research Study No. 1? Or from other postulates of the same general character?

18. Gordon follows the author of Accounting Research Study No. 1 in continuing the narrow application of the word "pragmatic." Is it necessary to "imagine any other meaning" for the word? Would a reading of the writings of the "pragmatists," especially Peirce, Dewey, James, and Lewis reveal an original and broader meaning of the term? Did the pragmatic philosophy suffer

by lack of "operational" concepts, or was operationalism (in the sense that a meaning for a concept was determined by reference to consequences of its employment) at the heart of the pragmatic viewpoint?

19. What is Gordon's distinction between the "direct" and the "indirect" influence of the use of particular accounting-treatment rules on a firm's future receipts? Is his denial of any direct influence analogous to the proposition that retained earnings is not a source of cash, or that the balance of the cash account does not necessarily determine the amount of cash on hand?

20. In Gordon's hypothesis of the role of financial statements in investment-disinvestment decisions by stockholders, does he specify how a stockholder's conclusion that the corporation under consideration is "doing well" enters into a judgment about "the future prospects" of the corporation? Is Gordon referring to a present role of financial statements or to a possible role under modified reporting? Does Gordon's analysis sufficiently emphasize the stockholders' concern with the shifting of investments among companies? Is maximization of the wealth of a particular firm necessarily in the interest of present stockholders? In the social interest?

21. Does Gordon's hypothesis about the role of financial statements in investment-disinvestment decisions of stockholders assume that stockholder-action can effectively change Management? May a decline in the inclination to invest in a particular company's shares be reflected in a lower price for the outstanding shares, and a higher effective cost to the corporation on the issuance of new shares? Is there a financial reporting problem from the viewpoint of stockholders even if, say, concerted stockholder-action is hindered by wide distribution of shares and inertia, and even if no effective action by stockholders toward the maximization of the wealth of the corporation may be expected in the foreseeable future?

22. Does Gordon's observation that "what has happened is an accounting determination" assert that the selection of things and measurements to serve as data depends on the identification of ends in view and on the adoption of means-consequences hypotheses?

23. Are findings or assumptions about the behavioral response of stockholders to financial reports prepared with the use of alterna-

tive accounting-treatment rules necessary for the adoption of criteria for choices among the treatment rules?

24. Gordon interpreted Anthony ("Showdown on Accounting Principles," *Harvard Business Review*, May/June 1963, p. 106) as accepting "the judgment of authoritative men of affairs" on the suitability of particular accounting-treatment rules as a condition of immediate specification of permissible treatment rules. Anthony associated the urgency for such immediate specification with the possibility that the Securities and Exchange Commission would impose its own accounting-treatment rules on listed corporations. Spacek ("A Suggested Solution to the Principles Dilemma," *The Accounting Review*, April 1964, pp. 275-284) also urged an early authoritative determination of standards, subject to future modification as subsequent debate and "reasoning" demonstrated the errors in the earlier determinations. How is the foregoing related to Baxter's distinction between "rules for action" and "principles" ("Recommendations on Accounting Theory," in *Studies in Accounting Theory*, ed. W. T. Baxter and Sidney Davidson, pp. 414-427)?

Bibliography

AMERICAN ACCOUNTING ASSOCIATION, *Accounting and Reporting Standards for Corporate Financial Statements and Preceding Statements and Supplements*. Madison, Wisconsin: American Accounting Association, 1957.

————, COMMITTEE ON CONCEPTS AND STANDARDS UNDERLYING CORPORATE FINANCIAL STATEMENTS, "Accounting and Reporting Standards for Corporate Financial Statements, 1957 Revision," *The Accounting Review*, October 1957, pp. 536-546.

————, "Price Level Changes and Financial Statements," *The Accounting Review*, October 1951, pp. 468-474.

————, "Reserves and Retained Income," *The Accounting Review*, April 1951, pp. 153-156.

————, EXECUTIVE COMMITTEE, "A Tentative Statement of Accounting Principles Affecting Corporate Reports," *The Accounting Review*, June 1936, pp. 187-191.

"American Institute Council Acts on Recommendation for Disclosure of Departures from APB Opinions; text of conclusions and recommendations of the Sepecial Committee on Opnions of the APB as amended and adopted by the Institute's Council," *The Journal of Accountancy*, November 1964, p. 12.

AMERICAN INSTITUTE OF ACCOUNTANTS, *Changing Concepts of Business Income*, Report of Study Group on Business Income. New York: The Macmillan Company, 1952.

————, COMMITTEE ON ACCOUNTING PROCEDURE, "Report of Committee on Terminology," *Accounting Research Bulletin No. 9 (Special)*. New York: American Institute of Accountants, 1941.

————, *Restatement and Revision of Accounting Research Bulletins*, Accounting Research Bulletin No. 43. New York: American Institute of Accountants, 1953.

AMERICAN INSTITUTE OF CERTIFIED PUBLIC ACCOUNTANTS, STAFF, "Comments on 'A Tentative Set of Broad Accounting Principles for Business Enterprises,'" *The Journal of Accountancy*, April 1963, pp. 36-48.

————, "Comments on 'The Basic Postulates of Accounting,'" *The Journal of Accountancy*, January 1963, pp. 44-55.

————, STAFF, ACCOUNTING RESEARCH DIVISION, *Reporting the Financial Effects of Price-Level Changes*, Accounting Research Study No. 6. New York: American Institute of Certified Public Accountants, 1963.

ANTHONY, ROBERT N., "Showdown on Accounting Principles," *Harvard Business Review*, May/June 1963, pp. 99-106.

ANTON, HECTOR R., "Some Aspects of Measurement and Accounting," *Journal of Accounting Research*, Vol. 2, No. 1, Spring 1964, pp. 1-9.

ARISTOTLE, *The Organon*, trans. by Harold P. Cooke and others, 2 vols. Cambridge, Mass.: Harvard University Press, 1938.

ARTHUR ANDERSEN & CO., *The Postulate of Accounting—What It Is, How It Is Determined, How It Should Be Used*. Subject File AC 320, Item 2. Chicago: Arthur Andersen & Co., 1960.

AUSTIN, J. L., *Sense and Sensibilia*, reconstructed from the manuscript notes by G. J. Warnock. Oxford: The Clarendon Press, 1962.

"Authority of the Accounting Principles Board," editorial, *The Journal of Accountancy*, March 1964, pp. 33, 34.

AYER, A. J., *The Problem of Knowledge*. Baltimore: Penguin Books, Inc., 1956.

BAXTER, W. T., ed., *Studies in Accounting*. London: Sweet & Maxwell, 1950.

————, AND SIDNEY DAVIDSON, ed., *Studies in Accounting Theory*. Homewood, Ill.: Richard D. Irwin, Inc., 1962.

BEDFORD, NORTON M., "Management Motives in Accounting Measurements," *Quarterly Review of Economics and Business*, Autumn 1963, pp. 35-45.

————, AND VAHE BALADOUNI, "A Communication Theory Approach to Accountancy," *The Accounting Review*, October 1962, pp. 650-659.

————, AND NICHOLAS DOPUCH, "Research Methodology and Accounting Theory—Another Perspective," *The Accounting Review*, July 1961, pp. 351-361.

BIERMAN, HAROLD, JR., "Measurement and Accounting," *The Accounting Review*, July 1963, pp. 501-507.

BOULDING, KENNETH E., *Reconstruction of Economics*. New York: John Wiley & Sons, Inc., 1950.

BRIDGMAN, P. W., *The Logic of Modern Physics*. New York: The Macmillan Company, 1928.

BRUNDAGE, PERCIVAL F., "Milestones on the Path of Accounting," *Harvard Business Review*, July 1951, pp. 71-81.

CANNING, JOHN B., *The Economics of Accountancy*. New York: The Ronald Press Company, 1929.

CANNON, ARTHUR M., "Discussion Notes on 'The Basic Postulates of Accounting,'" *The Journal of Accountancy*, February 1962, pp. 42-53.

CARNAP, RUDOLF, *The Nature and Application of Inductive Logic*, consisting of six sections from Logical Foundations of Probability. Chicago: University of Chicago Press, 1950.

CASTELL, ALBUREY, *An Introduction to Modern Philosophy in Six Philosophical Problems*. New York: The Macmillan Company, 1943.

CHAMBERS, R. J., "Blueprint for a Theory of Accounting," *Accounting Research*, Vol. 6, 1955, pp. 17-25.

———, "The Conditions of Research in Accounting," *The Journal of Accountancy*, December 1960, pp. 33-39.

———, "Details for a Blueprint," *The Accounting Review*, April 1957, pp. 206-215.

———, "Measurement and Objectivity in Accounting," *The Accounting Review*, April 1964, pp. 264-274.

———, *The Resolution of Some Paradoxes in Accounting*, Occasional Paper No. 2. Vancouver 8: The University of British Columbia, 1963.

———, *Towards a General Theory of Accounting*. Adelaide, Australia: The University of Adelaide, 1961.

———, "Why Bother with Postulates?" *Journal of Accounting Research*, Vol. 1, No. 1, Spring 1963, pp. 3-15.

COHEN, MORRIS R., AND ERNEST NAGEL, *An Introduction to Logic and Scientific Method*. New York: Harcourt, Brace & World, Inc., 1934.

DEIN, RAYMOND C., "A Glance Backward at Research in Accounting," *The Accounting Review*, January 1961, pp. 1-8.

———, "Price Level Adjustments: Fetish in Accounting," *The Accounting Review*, January 1955, pp. 3-24.

———, "Price Level Adjustments: Rejoinder to Professor Husband," *The Accounting Review*, January 1956, pp. 58-63.

DEINZER, HARVEY T., *The American Accounting Association-Sponsored Statements of Standards for Corporate Financial Reports, A Perspective*, Accounting Series No. 3. Gainesville, Florida: College of Business Administration, University of Florida, 1964.

DE ROOVER, RAYMOND, "The Lingering Influence of Medieval Practices," *The Accounting Review*, April 1943, pp. 148-151.

————, "New Perspectives on the History of Accounting," *The Accounting Review*, July 1955, pp. 405-420.

DESCARTES, RENÉ, "Discourse on Method," in *Man and the Universe: The Philosophers of Science*, ed. Saxe Commins and Robert N. Linscott, pp. 159-216. New York: Random House, Inc., 1947.

DEVINE, CARL T., "Research Methodology and Accounting Theory Formation," *The Accounting Review*, July 1960, pp. 387-399.

DEWEY, JOHN, *Logic, The Theory of Inquiry.* New York: Holt, Rinehart and Winston, Inc., 1938.

———— *Reconstruction in Philosophy,* 1920 edition with a new introduction by the author. Boston: The Beacon Press, 1948.

———— *Theory of Valuation.* Reprinted from International Encyclopedia of Unified Science, Vol. II, No. 4. Chicago: University of Chicago Press, 1939.

————, AND ARTHUR F. BENTLEY, *Knowing and the Known.* Boston: The Beacon Press, 1949.

EDWARDS, EDGAR O., AND PHILIP W. BELL, *The Theory and Measurement of Business Income.* Berkeley and Los Angeles: University of California Press, 1961.

FISHER, IRVING, *The Nature of Capital and Income.* New York: The Macmillan Company, 1912.

FRANK, PHILIPP, *Modern Science and Its Philosophy.* Cambridge: Harvard University Press, 1949.

FULLER, B. A. G., *A History of Philosophy,* rev. ed., 2 vols. New York: Holt, Rinehart and Winston, Inc., 1945.

GORDON, MYRON J., "Postulates, Principles and Research in Accounting," *The Accounting Review*, April 1964, pp. 251-263.

GRADY, PAUL, "Outline for Inventory of Generally Accepted Accounting Principles for Business Enterprises," *The Journal of Accountancy*, November 1963, pp. 52-55.

————, "Quest for Accounting Principles," *The Journal of Accountancy*, May 1962, pp. 45-50.

HANDY, ROLLO, AND PAUL KURTZ, "A Current Appraisal of the Behavioral Sciences: Preferential Behavior," *The American Behavioral Scientist*, Supplement, March 1954, pp. 121-136.

HILL, THOMAS M., "An Analysis of Supplementary Statement No. 2," *The Accounting Review*, January 1952, pp. 16-24.

HOMBURGER, RICHARD H., "Study of History—Gateway to Perspective," *The Accounting Review*, July 1958, pp. 501-503.

HUSBAND, GEORGE R., "Accounting Postulates: An Analysis of the Tentative Statement of Accounting Principles," *The Accounting Review*, December 1937, pp. 386-401.

———, "The Corporate-Entity Fiction and Accounting Theory," *The Accounting Review*, September 1938, pp. 241-253.

———, "Professor Dein, Mr. Alexander, and Supplementary Statement No. 2," *The Accounting Review*, July 1955, pp. 383-399.

IVES, KENNETH, "The Nature of the Accounting Unit," *The Accounting Review*, October 1951, pp. 516-517.

JACKSON, J. HUGH, "Present Tendencies in Business Education," *The Journal of Accountancy*, November 1927, pp. 346-359.

JAMES, WILLIAM, *Pragmatism*. New York: Meridian Books, Inc., 1907.

JENNINGS, ALVIN R., "Present Day Challenges in Financial Reporting," *The Journal of Accountancy*, January 1958, pp. 28-34.

JOACHIM, HAROLD H., *The Nature of Truth, An Essay*. Oxford: The Clarendon Press, 1906.

JONES, RALPH C., *Effects of Price Level Changes on Business Income, Capital, and Taxes*. Columbus, Ohio: American Accounting Association, 1956.

KANT, IMMANUEL, *Critique of Pure Reason*, trans. by F. Max Müller, rev. 2d ed. New York: The Macmillan Company, 1924.

KEYNES, JOHN NEVILLE, *The Scope and Method of Political Economy*. New York: Kelley & Millman, Inc., 1955.

KOHLER, E. L., "Why Not Retain Historical Cost?", *The Journal of Accountancy*, October 1963, pp. 35-41.

LANGER, CLARENCE, "Paciolo—Patriarch of Accounting," *The Accounting Review*, July 1958, pp. 482-484.

LITTLEFIELD, W. JOSEPH, "Research Program of Controllers Institute Research Foundation," *The Accounting Review*, January 1961, pp. 32-35.

LITTLETON, A. C., *Accounting Evolution to 1900*. New York: American Institute Publishing Company, 1933.

———, "Accounting Research Study No. 1," a book review, *The Accounting Review*, July 1962, pp. 602-605.

———, "Accounting Research Study No. 3," a book review, *The Accounting Review*, January 1963, pp. 220-222.

———, "Choice Among Alternatives," *The Accounting Review*, July 1956, pp. 363-370.

———, *Structure of Accounting Theory*. Urbana, Illinois: American Accounting Association, 1953.

————, "Tests for Principles," *The Accounting Review*, March 1938, pp. 16-24.

————, AND B. S. YAMEY, ed., *Studies in the History of Accounting*. London: Sweet and Maxwell, 1956.

————, AND V. K. ZIMMERMAN, *Accounting Theory: Continuity and Change*. Englewood Cliffs, N. J.: Prentice-Hall, Inc., 1962.

LOCKE, JOHN, *An Essay Concerning Human Understanding*, collated and annotated by Alexander Campbell Fraser, 2 vols. Oxford: The Clarendon Press, 1894.

MCFARLAND, WALTER B., "Research in Management Accounting by the National Association of Accountants," *The Accounting Review*, January 1961, pp. 21-25.

MATTESSICH, RICHARD, *Accounting and Analytical Methods*. Homewood, Ill.: Richard D. Irwin, Inc., 1964.

————, "Mathematical Models in Business Accounting," *The Accounting Review*, July 1958, pp. 472-481.

MAUTZ, R. K., "Accounting as a Social Science," *The Accounting Review*, April 1963, pp. 317-325.

MAY, GEORGE O., *Financial Accounting: A Distillation of Experience*, rev. 1961. New York: The Macmillan Company, 1961.

————, *Twenty-Five Years of Accounting Responsibility, 1911-1936*, Bishop Carleton Hunt, ed. New York: Price, Waterhouse & Co., 1936.

MILL, JOHN STUART, *A System of Logic*, 8th ed. New York: Harper & Row, Publishers, 1884.

MOONITZ, MAURICE, *The Basic Postulates of Accounting*, Accounting Research Study No. 1. New York: American Institute of Certified Public Accountants, 1961.

————, "Why Do We Need 'Postulates' and 'Principles'?" *The Journal of Accountancy*, December 1963, pp. 42-46.

NAGEL, ERNEST, *The Structure of Science. Problems in the Logic of Scientific Explanations*. New York: Harcourt, Brace & World, Inc., 1961.

NELSON, EDWARD G., "Science and Accounting," *The Accounting Review*, October 1949, pp. 354-359.

NISSLEY, WARREN W., "Education for the Profession of Accountancy," *The Journal of Accountancy*, August 1935, pp. 90-103.

PATON, WILLIAM ANDREW, *Accounting Theory*. Chicago: A.S.P. Accounting Studies Press, Ltd., 1962.

————, AND A. C. LITTLETON, *An Introduction to Corporate Account-*

ing Standards. Chicago: American Accounting Association, 1940.

PELOUBET, MAURICE E., "Is Further Uniformity Desirable or Possible?" *The Journal of Accountancy,* April 1961, pp. 35-41.

POWELL, WELDON, "Report on the Accounting Research Activities of the American Institute of Certified Public Accountants," *The Accounting Review,* January 1961, pp. 26-31.

PRINCE, THOMAS R., *Extension of the Boundaries of Accounting Theory.* Cincinnati: South-Western Publishing Company, 1963.

"Proposal to Council Would Define Authority of APB Pronouncements," editorial, *The Journal of Accountancy,* April 1964, pp. 9-12.

QUEENAN, JOHN W., "Postulates: Their Place in Accounting Research," *The Journal of Accountancy,* August 1962, pp. 24-33.

RATNER, JOSEPH, ed., *Intelligence in the Modern World,* "Introduction to John Dewey's Philosophy." New York: Random House, Inc., 1939.

"Report to Council of the Special Committee on Research Program," *The Journal of Accountancy,* December 1958, pp. 62-68.

RIPLEY, WILLIAM Z., *Main Street and Wall Street.* Boston: Little, Brown & Company, 1927.

RUSSELL, BERTRAND, *An Inquiry into Meaning and Truth.* New York: W. W. Norton & Company, Inc., 1940.

———, *My Philosophical Development.* London: George Allen & Unwin, Ltd., 1959.

———, *The Problems of Philosophy.* New York: Holt, Rinehart and Winston, Inc., 1912.

RYLE, GILBERT, *Dilemmas.* Cambridge: The University Press, 1954.

SALTER, LEONARD A., *A Critical Review of Research in Land Economics.* Minneapolis: University of Minnesota Press, 1948.

SCOTT, DR, "The Tentative Statement of Principles," *The Accounting Review,* September 1937, pp. 296-303.

SELLARS, R. W., *The Essentials of Philosophy.* New York: The Macmillan Company, 1924.

SPACEK, LEONARD, "Are Accounting Principles Generally Accepted?" *The Journal of Accountancy,* April 1961, pp. 41-46.

———, "The Need for an Accounting Court," *The Accounting Review,* July 1958, pp. 368-379.

———, "A Suggested Solution to the Principles Dilemma," *The Accounting Review,* April 1964, pp. 275-284.

SPROUSE, ROBERT T., "The 'Radically Different' Principles of Accounting Research Study No. 3," *The Journal of Accountancy*, May 1964, pp. 63-69.

————, AND MAURICE MOONITZ, *A Tentative Set of Broad Accounting Principles for Business Enterprises*, Accounting Research Study No. 3. New York: American Institute of Certified Public Accountants, 1962.

STANS, MAURICE, "AAA Proposals Offer Practical Suggestions for Dealing with Price Level Changes in Accounting," *The Journal of Accountancy*, January 1952, pp. 52-59.

STAUBUS, GEORGE J., "Comments on Accounting and Reporting Standards for Corporate Financial Statements—1957 Revision," *The Accounting Review*, January 1958, pp. 11-24.

————, "The Residual Equity Point of View in Accounting," *The Accounting Review*, January 1959, pp. 3-13.

STOREY, REED K., "Accounting Principles: AAA and AICPA," *The Journal of Accountancy*, June 1964, pp. 47-55.

————, *The Search for Accounting Principles: Today's Problems in Perspective*. New York: American Institute of Certified Public Accountants, Inc., 1964.

A STUDY GROUP AT THE UNIVERSITY OF ILLINOIS, CENTER FOR INTERNATIONAL EDUCATION AND RESEARCH IN ACCOUNTING, *A Statement of Basic Accounting Postulates and Principles*. Urbana, Illinois: The Board of Trustees of the University of Illinois, 1964.

SWEENEY, HENRY W., *Stabilized Accounting*. New York: Harper & Row, Publishers, 1936.

THAYER, H. S., *The Logic of Pragmatism*. New York: Humanities Press, Inc., 1952.

VAIHINGER, HANS, *The Philosophy of 'As-If,'* trans. by C. K. Ogden. New York: Harcourt, Brace & World, Inc., 1925.

VANCE, LAWRENCE L., "The Authority of History in Inventory Valuation," *The Accounting Review*, July 1943, pp. 219-227.

VATTER, WILLIAM J., "Another Look at the 1957 Statement," *The Accounting Review*, October 1962, pp. 660-669.

————, "Postulates and Principles," *Journal of Accounting Research*, Vol. 1, No. 2, Autumn 1963, pp. 188-197.

WEINBERG, JULIUS RUDOLPH, *An Examination of Logical Positivism*. London: Routledge & Kegan Paul, Ltd., 1936.

WHITE, MORTON, *The Age of Analysis*. New York: New American Library of World Literature, Inc., 1955.

WILLIAMS, THOMAS H. AND CHARLES H. GRIFFIN, *The Mathematical Di-*

mension of Accountancy. Cincinnati: Southwestern Publishing Co., 1964.

WITSCHEY, ROBERT E., "The Business Need for Better Accounting Principles," *The Journal of Accountancy,* January 1964, pp. 27-31.

————, "Response to Article by Robert N. Anthony on 'Showdown on Accounting Principles,'" *Harvard Business Review,* September/October 1963, pp. 35-36. Reprinted in *The Journal of Accountancy,* November 1963, pp. 68, 69.

Index

Absolute idealism, 34
Academic thinking vs. practical thinking, 157
Accounting
  a priori part of, 109
  Accrual Basis, 12
  Cash Basis, 12
  central purpose of, 94
  contributions, 94
  corporate, 74, 76-77
  curricula for, 1, 4, 14, 159
  empirical part of, 109
  history of: early, 1-3; since 1900, 9-13, 145
  management, 155-156
  objectives of, 76, 107, 115
  practicing area of, 9, 14, 28, 85
  schools of, 14
  stabilized, 12
  teachers of, 20, 21
  unifying force within, 114
  utilization-of-resources, 77, 81
Accounting Court, 113, 152-154
Accounting data, bases of, Postulate Y-2, 124
Accounting identity, Postulate Y-1, 124
Accounting narrative, 10-12
Accounting practices (see Practices)
Accounting principles (see Principles)
Accounting Principles Board
  currrent mode of operation, 147
  diversity in practices, reduction of, 3
  long-range research program, 148
  majority positions of, 154
  and 1959 demands for constructive action, 20, 131
  Opinion No. 2, 154
  principles, establishment of, acceptance function for, 105-107, 146
  and quest for certainty, 100
  Spacek's proposal based on action of, 153-154
Accounting Procedure Committee

ad hoc approach of, 112, 144, 147
  availability of, prior to 1938, 19
  operating performance doctrine, 80
  recognition of, in shaping principles, 20
  reconstitution of, 19
Accounting profession, 11, 17, 20, 73-74
  agreement within, problem of reaching, 155
  authoritative position within, 154
  education for, 13-14
  and Securities and Exchange Commission, 19
  financial reporting and, 35; See also Financial reports
  obstacles to advance of, 112
Accounting propositions
  action, 126
  basic, 1936 Statement on, 77-82
  coherence theory of truth, 41
  directive, precedent approach to, 153-154
  and postulates, association of, accounting theory as, 108
  scientific method for inquiry into, standard of, 29
  validity of, interrelatedness as criterion of, 57, 142
  warrantability of, 3-4, 21, 27, 29, 89
Accounting reports
  functional character of, Postulate Z-5, 125
  See also Financial reports
Accounting research (see Research)
Accounting Research Bulletins, 11, 20, 43, 107, 109, 147, 148
Accounting Research Study No. 1, 21, 54, 75, 105-117
  compatibility requirement, 127-128
  interpretations of, 111-117
  postulates, 21, 108-117, 145, 153
  principles, basis for deducing, 123
  problem-oriented approach, 129
  value, relative emphasis on, 122

Accounting Research Study No. 6, 98
Accounting Research Study No. 3, 21, 54, 75, 96, 107, 122-134, 156
  interpretation difficulties, 129-134
  proposals, 146-147
  value, relative emphasis on, 145
Accounting Series Release 4, 19, 20
Accounting standards (*see* Standards)
Accounting statements (*see* Financial statements)
Accounting Terminology Committee, 37
Accounting theory (*see* Theory)
Accounting-treatment rules
  Accounting Procedure Committee influence on, 19-20
  of Accounting Research Study No. 3, 128: independent technical evaluation of, need for, 134, 146
  approaches to: Accounting Research Study No. 1, 115; case-by-case, 154; cost, 128; "new," 105-117, 122-134; postulates-broad-principles, 107-108, 128, 141
  authoritative, 153
  competing, 129
  detailed character of, 132
  as function of political and economic conditions, 154
  hypothesis testing of, 75
  justification for, 28
  relation of: to economic and social conditions, 142; to principles, 107
  selection of, experienced judgment and, 44, 145
  statistical, 154-155
Acquisition-price-aggregate, 38, 78, 91-92, 96
Action proposals, 126
Affirmation-negation, 39
Aggregate
  acquisition-price, 38, 78, 91-92, 96
  asset, 133
  entity and, 88
Agreement(s)
  industry-by-industry, 154-155
  interpersonal, 40, 44
  principles by, 56, 77, 110, 154-155
Allocation, 91, 92
  emphasis on valuation, 145
  entity in, neutrality of, 96

of historical costs, 77-80, 91, 95, 97-99, 144
  income tax, 41, 106
  objectivity of, 91
  as premise for standards, 73-82, 85-100
  price-level adjustments and, 85, 97-100
  rationale of, 144
American Accounting Association, 9, 14, 17-18, 75, 98, 108
  Paton-Littleton monograph published by, 9, 19, 54, 56, 76, 82, 85, 94, 108, 144
  research effort of, 18-19
  Statements sponsored by, 107, 144, 148, 158: 1936 Statement, 9, 17, 19-21, 75-82, 85, 95, 143-144
American Institute of Accountants, 11, 17, 19-20
American Institute of Certified Public Accountants, 3
  Accounting Research Division of, Staff of, 98
  Council of, 106, 144, 153-154
  Director of Accounting Research, 106, 147-148
  diversity in practices, 3, 152
  "new" approach to accounting-treatment rules, 105-117, 122-134
  price-level-adjustment study sponsored by, 98
  research study by, 19-21, 105-117, 127, 144: present direction of, 134, 145-148
Andersen (Arthur) & Company, 153
Antecedent, 10: Postulate X-4 on, 124, 130
Anton, Hector R., 124
Argument
  full critical, 153
  persuasive, 77
  reductibility, 43
Aristotle, 34-35, 46, 53
"As if" propositions, 92
Assertions, warranted, 51-52
  postulate tests for, 75, 129
Asset aggregate, 133
Asset-changes, enterprise, 88
Assets, revaluation of, 11-12
Assignment of changes, Postulate B-4, 130
Associations, psychological
  explanation and, 13
  immediate, 153, 155
Assumption, 107
  "simple-minded," 128

Attest function, 159
Axioms
    assumption as equivalent to, 107
    Chambers' suggestions for, 57
    debatable criteria for, 27
    postulates and, 107, 111
    and principles, 147
    scientific method and, 45
    squeezing of, 142
Ayer, A. J., 41, 43

Baconian conception of induction, 50
Balance sheet, 13, 78, 82, 158
    See also Financial statements
Bedford, Norton, 57, 73, 143
Behavior, 35-36
Bell, Philip W., 155
Beneficiaries, Postulate Y-3, 124
Bentley, Arthur F., 35-36
Berkeley, George, 42-43
Bierman, Harold, Jr., 134
Bond discount, 78
Bookkeeping, double-entry, 2, 12, 48
Boole, George, 46
Boulding, Kenneth E., 156
Bridgman, P. W., 44, 47

Canning, J. B., 56
Cannon, Arthur M., 112-113
Capital, contributed, 81-82
Capital stock and surplus, changes
    in, 81
Capitalism, 12, 38
    expansion of, double-entry book-
        keeping and, 48
Carnap, Rudolf, 43, 51
Cartesian coordinates, 8
Cash-flow analyses, 89
Causation, 3, 47
Certainty
    degrees of, 95
    quest for, 40, 53
Chambers, R. J., 45, 57, 87, 89, 91,
    93, 134, 142-145
Cohen, Morris, 30-32
Coherence, 28, 41, 52, 146
    hypothesis as exhibiting, 52
    theory of, 57, 146
Common law, 152
Communication
    as additional postulate, 115
    organ of, 20
    theory of, 28, 57
Comparison-contrast, 33
Conception
    clear and distinct, 40
    controlling or direct, 10, 33, 37,
        38, 44, 88, 110, 123
    integrated, 86, 89

Concepts
    implications from, 95
    operational meanings of, 47
    persuasive, 113
    theory and, 89
    underlying, 85-97
Consequences
    as accounting-practice guides, 114
    differential, 33, 155
    evaluated, 127
    expected, 99, 154
    flowing from data, 44
    historical, 10
    hypotheses involving, absence of,
        97, 111
    independent of particular ends
        sought, 144
    means-, 13, 38, 45, 109, 110, 114-
        116, 123, 143, 157
    observed, 34
    postulated, 47, 49, 123
Consideration, measured, 91-92, 94,
    96
Considerations, normative, 143
Consistency
    end in view and, 125
    Postulate Z-3, 125
    in scientific method, 44
Contingent relation, deductive im-
    plications and, 46
Contract, institution of, 73
Contributed capital, 81-82
Contributions accounting, 94
Controllers, 20
Controllers Institute Research Foun-
    dation, 18
Conventional ordering of figures,
    Postulate Y-2, 124
Conventions, 76
Cooperative efforts, Postulate X-3,
    124
Corporate financial statements, 156
Correlations, familiar, 44
Co-respondence theory, 51
Cosmology, 34-35, 53
Cost absorption doctrine, 79
Cost pricing, 41
Cost theory of value, 96
Costs
    acquisition-price aggregate, 38, 78,
        91-92, 96
    allocation of (see Allocation)
    charged-off, reinstatement of, 80
    current, 41, 97
    diminutions or expiration of, 78
    and entity concept, 87, 91
    flow of, 91, 99
    full, reasoning in, 94
    of future income, 78

historical (*see* Historical costs)
hypotheses in terms of, 127
production, value-in-exchange, 93
recapture of, 93
recoverability of, 79, 93
replacement, 122
and revenues, 94
unamortized, 78-79, 91
variable, 94
Costs attach notice, 92-93, 96, 122
Creditor-protection interest, 12

Data, 36-39
  accounting, bases of, Postulate
    Y-2, 124
  collection and arrangement of, 37,
    44-45
  completely scientific, 95
  discriminated, 44
  existential, interactions among, 40
  objectivity of, 96
  quantitative, Postulate A-1, 126
  relevance of, 31, 73, 74, 112
  sense-, 36-37, 43-44
Deduction, 27-28, 50
  implementation and, 131
Deductive reasoning, 99, 111
Deductive systems, 45, 48, 127, 143,
    156
Definition(s)
  extension of, 129
  in Greek logic, 53
  of logic, need for, 46
  meanings as, 33
Dein, Raymond C., 99
Deinzer, Harvey T., 75
Depreciation
  accelerated, 41
  deductions for, 12
  replacement-cost, 41
deRoover, Raymond, 2
Descartes, 39-40
Devine, Carl T., 45, 57, 73, 143
Dewey, John, 29, 30, 32-39, 41-42,
    44-53, 110, 115-116, 123, 126,
    142, 156
Discourse, 38, 45
Dopuch, Nicholas, 57, 73, 143
Double-entry bookkeeping, 2, 12
  modern capitalism and, 48

Earned surplus, 81-82
Earning power, 90
Economic theory, family, 38
Eduction, process of, 53
Edwards, Edgar O., 155
Empiricism, 38-45
  logical, 47
  traditional, 34, 40-43, 47, 56

End in view
  absence of, in Accounting Re-
    search Study No. 1, 111
  as aspect of adjustive behavior, 35
  postulates dependent on, 108
  recognition of, by Bedford and
    Dopuch, 143
  relation of: to consistency, 125; to
    fiction, 93; to inquiry process,
    37-38, 44, 49, 110, 116, 126-
    127, 157
Entity
  concept of: costs and, 87, 91; in
    1936 Statement, 78
  in cost allocation, neutrality of, 96
  enterprise asset-changes, 88
  explanation of, 126
  identification of, 88
  Paton and Littleton discussion of,
    87-89
Epistemologies, 34, 142
Equilibrium, 39, 156
Equities, balancing of, 73
Equity
  residual, 89
  stockholders', changes in, 82
Evaluation criteria, 76
Events
  in Dewey's theory of inquiry, 36
  experienced, 43
  irreducible, 52
Evolutionary development, 3, 4, 56
  deterrent influences, 112
  healthy, fostering of, 112
  as justification for current prac-
    tices, 3, 4, 141, 145, 157
Exchange
  money, 92
  process of, Postulate A-2, 126
  value-in, production cost and, 93
Exchangeability, 124, 126
  See also Value
Existences, 88
  objective, 123, 128
Existential operations, 46, 52
Existential possibilities, 33, 39, 45,
    47, 50, 111, 143
Experience, 37, 42, 48
  conventions derived from, 76
  in Dewey's theory of inquiry, 44,
    51
  observation by, 36, 125, 145-148
  organizing, 39
  ultimate, 43, 44, 51-52
  as validating theories, 28, 40-41
Experiment, controlled, 32, 36, 38,
    48, 123
Experimentalism in scientific method,
    48-51

Factual premisses, 43, 52
Fairness, 110, 116, 153
Familiar correlations, 44
Fantasy, 39, 93
Fictions, 93, 96
Financial reports
    comparability of, 154
    corporate, 156
    factual plane for, 158
    legal requirements for, 81
    problem of, 35
    provisional, 90
    relevance as goal of, 158-159
    standards of, 105
Financial statements
    articulation of, 130
    balance sheet, 13, 78, 82, 158
    corporate, 156
    credence for, 112
    general-purpose concept of, 157
    income (see Income statement)
    periodic, necessity for, 90
    Postulate B-1 definition of, 130
First Cause, concept of, 4
First-in-first-out (FIFO) inventory
    method, 11
Foundation propositions (see Postu-
    lates)
Frank, Philipp, 47, 51
Fund-flow analyses, 89
Fundamentalness, 100, 106-108, 114-
    115, 127-128, 145
Future receivables and payables, dis-
    counting of, 122

Generalization
    about accounting practice, 56-57,
        142, 145-146
    in Baconian conception of induc-
        tion, 50
Grady, Paul, 148
Greek culture, classic, 132
Greek influence on modern thought,
    52-54
Greek logic and science, 34, 46, 53
Greer, Howard C., 9

Handy, Rollo, 156
Hatfield, H. R., 4, 17, 18, 147
Herodotus, 31
Hill, Thomas, M., 97
Historical costs
    accelerated depreciation, 41
    allocation of, 77-80, 91, 95, 97-99,
        144: See also Allocation
    rationalization of, 146
    unamortized, value and, 77-78,
        87, 122
Historical judgment, 13

Historical premise, 10-12
Homburger, Richard H., 1
Homogeneity, 92, 96
Hume, David, 43
Husband, George, 79, 81, 88-89
Hypotheses
    as controlling conception, 33, 88
    in Dewey's theory of inquiry, 31-
        34, 37-38, 45, 48-51, 93, 116,
        123
    as exhibiting coherence, 52
    as goal, testing of, 75
    historical narrative as, 13
    by implication, 32
    involving consequences, absence
        of, 97, 111
    parasitic-disease, 49-50
    structure of, rejection of, 45
    in terms of cost, 13
Hypothesis-lines, alternative, 127

Ideal, 77, 81
    of one true accounting income,
        157
Idealism, absolute, 34
Ideas, 28
    coherence and, 52, 146
    deductive arrangement of, 45, 145
    in Dewey's theory of inquiry, 37,
        39
    extant, alternative sets of, 38
    guiding structure of, 20
    interrelated, framework of, 41
    origin and development of, 2-3
    signification function of, 43
    teams of, 38
Ideas-in-system, 40
Ideologies, 157
"If-then" propositions, 33, 34
Imperatives, 113, 124
Implementation, deduction and, 131
Implication(s)
    from concepts, selection of, 95
    deductive, 46, 127
    derivation of: from hypotheses,
        32; by squeezing, 32, 111, 123,
        142
    mathematics as aid in developing,
        143
    necessary, 32, 40, 46, 144
    of postulates, 129
Implicatory process, 131
Impressment, 48, 127
Inclusion-exclusion, 38, 110, 123
Income
    accounting, one true, ideal of, 157
    artificial stabilization of, 81
    distortion of, 81
    future, cost of, 78

net, 158
  objective, 89, 91, 94
Income analysis, national, 156
Income reporting, 12-13, 158
Income statement
  all-inclusive, 79-80
  connected series of statements, 80, 91
  functions of, 13, 90-91
  operations section of, 80
  present format of, 158
  prior, correction of, 80
  revised, 81
  sectional division of, 80
Income statistics, national, 12
Income tax allocation, 41, 106
Income tax laws, 10-12
Induction, 50-51
  Baconian conception of, 50
  deduction and, 28, 50
  observation as element in, 28, 50, 123
Inference, 31, 132-133
Input and output, proportionality of, 132
Inquiry, 28
  beginning of, 30-31, 35, 37
  behavioral, 157
  conceptual forms of, 32
  conceptual materials of, 37, 45, 49
  conjugate materials of, 39
  deductive phase of, 38, 45-46
  Dewey's theory of, 29, 30, 32 ff., 115, 123, 125, 142, 156
  dual aspects of, 36
  end in view, 37-38, 44, 49, 110, 116, 126-127, 157
  existential forms of, 32
  existential materials of, 37, 39-40, 45, 49
  fields of, axiomatization of, 27
  as form of behavior, 35-36
  hypotheses in, 31-34, 37-38, 45, 48-51, 93, 116, 123
  matrix of, 110
  object as product of, 33, 36, 38, 48, 49, 52, 116
  postulates in, function of, 28
  principles of, functional use of, 75, 110
  as process, 36-37, 39, 47, 75, 93, 126-127, 157: theory and, 142
  requirements of, in research efforts, 156-159
  social, Cartesian coordinates and space-time descriptions in, 36
  subject-matter of, 39, 49, 153
  successful, Postulate Z-3, 125
  termination of, 49, 116

Interactions
  as criteria for selection-rejection, 10, 32, 97, 111
  among existential data, 40
  mathematical models in, 48
  mutual, 13
  as possibilities, 33, 45, 50
  as working approximation, 36
Interactive complex, 133
Interactivities, 32, 122, 132
Interest, pooling of, 78, 88
Interests
  adjustment of, 74
  balancing of, 20
  diverse, reconciliation of, 73
  equitable alignment among, 73
  investor-protection emphasis, 13
  problems affecting, equitable resolution of, 74
  utilization-of-resources accounting, 77, 81
Interpreted mathematical systems, 45, 48, 127, 143, 156
Intuition, 10, 42, 47
Intuitive truths, 27
Inventory valuation
  FIFO, 11
  LIFO, 12, 13
  lower of cost or market, 78-79
Investor protection, 13

James, William, 47
Joachim, Harold H., 40-41, 52
Jones, Ralph C., 98
Judgment
  experienced, 44, 145
  historical, 13

Kant, Immanuel, 47
Kantianism, 34, 47
Keynes, John Neville, 50
Kinds
  in Dewey's theory of inquiry, 32-34
  systematic relations among, 75
Knowledge
  approaches to: axiomatic, 109, 111; postulational, 109, 111; problem, 110, 116, 157
  conditions for (see Inquiry; Scientific method)
  immediacy of, 45-48
  interpretation of, 27-28
Kohler, E. L., 85
Kurtz, Paul, 156

Langer, Clarence, 2
Last-in-first-out (LIFO) inventory method, 12, 13
Leases, long-term, 106, 113

Legal precedent, 152-154
Linear programming, 156
Linguistics, 44
Liquidation, 90
Littleton, A. C., 1
    book reviews, Accounting Re-
        search Studies, 112-114, 117,
        122
    coherence point of view of, 41, 52,
        146
    debate with Chambers, 57, 93
    evolutionary development doc-
        trine, 3, 145
    monograph with Paton, 9, 19, 54,
        56, 76, 82, 85, 89-91, 94, 108,
        144
    on practice, 56, 142
Locke, John, 41-43
Logic
    an antecedent foundation for
        mathematics, 46
    definition of term, need for, 46
    in Dewey's theory of inquiry, 29,
        32, 35, 46, 52-53
    Greek, 34-35, 46, 53
    Mill's system of, 52, 53
    plausible arguments and, 77
    symbolic, 46
Logical calculus, 47
Logical positivism, 51

Macroeconomics, 156
Market, 90, 96, 122, 132-133
Matching, 93-94, 99
Materiality as additional postulate,
    115
Mathematical operations, 92
Mathematical systems, 45-48, 127,
    143, 156
Mathematics
    as aid in developing implications,
        143
    as symbolization, 39, 45
    logic as foundation for, 46
    operations research and, 48
Mattessich, Richard, 45, 156
May, George O., 108
May Committee, 158
Meanings
    coherence and, 52
    as definitions, 33
Means-consequences, 13, 38, 45, 109,
    110, 114, 116, 123, 143, 157
Measurement
    of change, 130, 132-134
    objective, 122, 134
    rule of thumb, 134
    standards of, 132, 134
Mediation

    in Dewey's theory of inquiry, 38,
        45-48
    by professional accountants, 74
    proposition for Accounting Series
        Research Study No. 3, 129, 131
Metaphysical doctrines, rejection of,
    36, 45
Microeconomic theory, 28, 156
Mill, John Stuart, 50, 52-53
Moonitz, Maurice, 128, 130
Moore, G. E., 43
Moore, U., 17-18, 147

Nagel, Ernest, 29-32
National Accounting Association, 18
National Industrial Recovery Act, 11
New York Stock Exchange, 18, 20
Normative considerations, 143
Noumena, 47

Objective criteria, 43
Objective evidence, verifiable, 95-96
Objectivity, 13
    accountants' attitude toward, 134
    complete and conclusive, 95
    of cost allocation, 91
    of data, doctrine of, 96
Observation
    of controlled operations, 48
    as element in induction, 28, 50,
        123
    by experience, 36, 125, 145-148
Operating performance doctrine, 80
Operating reserves, 81
Operations
    controlled, observation of, 48
    in Dewey's theory of inquiry, 33,
        37, 47, 95
    empirical, 35
    existential, 46, 52
    mathematical, 92
    technical, significance of, 132
Operations research, 48
Opinion, unqualified, 74, 154
Output and input, proportionality of,
    132

Paciolo, Luca, 2
Paid-in capital and surplus, 81
Paton, W. A., 107-108, 122
    monograph with Littleton, 9, 19,
        54, 56, 76, 82, 85, 89-91, 94,
        108, 144
Peirce, Charles, 47, 116
Pension plans, 113
Percepts, 43, 44, 51
Phenomena, noumena and, 47
Plant appreciation problem, 11, 12
Pooling of interest, 78, 88

Possibilities, existential, 33, 39, 45, 47, 50, 111, 143
Postulated means-characteristic, 49
Postulates
  A-2 and B-2, 145
  acceptance of, bases for, 75
  of Accounting Research Study No. 1, 21, 108-117, 145, 153
  alternative set of, 123-126: X-group, 124; Y-group, 124-125; Z-group, 125
  assumption as equivalent to, 107
  axioms and, 107, 111
  broad principles in, 111, 123-129
  C-, 114, 117
  Chambers' suggestions for, 57, 142, 144
  continuity, 124, 130: breadth of concept, 96; Paton and Littleton concept of, 89-91; realization doctrine and, 132
  dovetailing of, 115
  early uses of term, 107
  end in view and, 108
  of fairness, 153
  fundamentalness attributes of, 100, 106-108, 114-115, 127-128, 145
  implications of, 129
  implications deductively derived from, 127
  in inquiry, function of, 28
  inter-postulate of profit-attributable-to-entire-process, 131
  logical structure of, 113
  multi-, 153
  and propositions, 108
  re-examination of, in research, 75
  self-evidence and, 113, 115, 130
  single-direction movement of, 113, 115, 127, 129-132
  structure of, 127
  tests for warranted assertions and, 75, 129
Postulational approach
  of Accounting Research Studies, 147, 153
  Cannon's justification of, 112-113
  to knowledge, 109, 111
  to standards, 107-108
Practices
  and community and business needs, functional relationship between, 158
  consequences as guides to, 114
  diversity in, reduction of, 3, 74, 112, 141, 152
  evaluation of, 75, 146

flexibility in, 74, 79: Postulate Z-1, 125
  generalization about, 56-57, 142, 145-146
  good, discrimination of, coherence theory for, 57, 146
  identification of, discovery of accounting principles and, 148
  justification of, 3, 4, 141, 145-146, 157
  rationale of, 145, 153
  Securities and Exchange Commission and, 17
  segmentation of, 89
  significance of, 4, 28, 146-147
  theory and, 28, 157
Practicing professional accountants, 19, 20, 28, 73, 74, 146
Pragmatism, 109, 114, 116
Precedent, 152-154
Price level
  adjustments in: AICPA study on, 98; cost-allocation doctrine and, 85, 97-100; reports on, 144
  changes in, 13, 79, 90: classification of, 133; effects of, Jones' report, 98
  exploration of, 144: problem in, Cannon's interpretation of, 113; reports on, mandatory, 97, 144
Principles
  acceptance function for, 105 ff., 146
  Accounting Procedure Committee, 20
  accounting-treatment rules, 107
  by agreement, 56, 77, 110, 154-155
  authoritative, Spacek's proposal for, 153
  axioms and, 147
  broad, 21, 107, 132-133, 145: basis for determining, 123; and postulates, 111, 123-129
  codification of, 21, 28, 37, 147
  development of: authoritative, 3, 153; axiomatic, 28, 109, 111, 142; empirical, 109; ethical, 109-110, 116; pragmatic, 109, 116; problem-oriented, 109-110, 129; rationalist, 109; sociological, 109-110, 116
  first, 47
  generally accepted, 20-21, 105, 107, 112, 144, 147
  identification of, definitional approach to, 115
  inventorying of, 21, 28, 37, 147-148

in Littleton's formulation, 146
and measurement rules, 134
in 1936 Statement, 77
postulates, single-direction movement of, 113, 115, 127, 129-132
in Institute's Research Program, 100, 105-107
Professional accountants, 19, 20, 28, 73, 74, 146
Professional management, 10
Pronouncements, 20, 147, 154
Propositions
accounting (see Accounting propositions)
scientific (see Inquiry; Scientific method)
Psychological associations, 13, 153, 155
Purchase, pooling of interest and, 78, 88
Purposive conduct, 4, 152-153

Qualitative attributes
Postulate X-1, 124, 126
Postulate X-2, 124
Qualitative situation in Dewey's theory of inquiry, 37-38
Quantitative data, Postulate A-1, 126

Rational action, 10, 128
Rationalism, 34, 38-42, 45, 47
Ratner, Joseph, 53
Realism, 99
naïve, 36
Realization doctrine, 91, 132
Reasoning, deductive, 99, 111
Recurring items, 80
Reductionism, 43-44
Replacement cost, 122
Research, 12-13, 17-26
AAA, major effort of, 18-19
Accounting Principles Board, long-range program of, 148
AIA, particularistic approach in, 19-20
AICPA, contemporary effort of, 19-21, 105-117, 127, 134, 144-148
character of, 18, 57
collection and arrangement of data as type of, 37, 44-45
and inquiry requirements, 156
new scientific outlook as standard for, 157
operations, 48
recommendation function of Special Committee on Research Program, 105
re-examination of postulates as goal of, 75
Reserves, 81
Resources, utilization of, 77, 81
Revenue, 86
and costs, functional relationship between, 94
Rules (see Accounting-treatment rules)
Russell, Bertrand, 35-37, 43-44, 46, 50-52
Ryle, Gilbert, 38, 41

Sanders, T. H., 17, 18, 147
Scientific method, 28-55
applicability of: to accounting materials, question of, 56-57; to social-field materials, recognition of, 95
axioms, relation of to, 45
circularity of, 44, 49
Cohen and Nagel on, 30-32
coherence in, 41
consistency in context of, 44: Postulate Z-3, 125
empiricism and, 40, 42-45, 47
experimentalism in, 48-51
Postulate Z-2, 125
rationalism and, 34, 38-42, 45, 47
self-correcting characteristic of, 44-45, 48-51
as standard for research, 157
value considerations, 29-30
See also Inquiry
Scott DR, 56, 78-79, 109
Securities and Exchange Commission, 11, 17-20, 80, 112, 141, 152
standards and (see Standards)
Selection-rejection, 10, 32, 37, 97, 111
Self-action, doctrine of, 36
Self-evidence, 113, 115, 130
Self-regulation, machinery of, 153
Sense-data, 36-37, 43-44
Sense-impressions, 42-43
Sensibilia, 36-37
Service potential, 92, 96
Shareholders (see Stockholders)
Similarities, 153, 155
"Simple-minded" assumptions, 128
Spacek, Leonard, 106, 110, 113, 116, 152-154
Space-time, 8, 36, 45, 47
Spectator theory, 53, 128
Standards
for AAA-sponsored statements, 76

consistent framework of, 86
cost-allocation doctrine as premise
for, 73-82, 85-100
establishment of, Spacek's view,
106
of financial reports, 105
formulation of: common-law analogy for, 152; concept for, 143;
main threads of, 21; postulated
approach to, 107-108
in 1936 Statement, 75-76
Paton and Littleton tests for, philosophical aspects of, 85
personal, 40
of scientific method, 29-30
source of, 20: agreement on, Securities and Exchange Commission and, 19
Stans, Maurice, 97
Statistical decision theory, 156
Stock dividends, 81
Stockholders, 74
absentee, 10
corporate dealings with, 80
information for, problem of, 155
protection of, emphasis on, 13
reports to, 155
Storey, Reed K., 148
Substance, 42, 47
Substantial authoritative support, 19
Surplus, 81-82
Sweeney, Henry W., 12
Syllogism, categorical, 46
Symbolic logic, 46
Symbols, 38-39, 45
Syntax, 43, 44

Technical operations, significance of,
132
Thayer, H. S., 35, 51
Theory
coherence, 57, 146
coherent body of, 76, 88
of communication, 28, 57
comprehensive, 77
concepts and, 89
co-respondence, 51
in Dewey's theory of inquiry, 41,
46, 49, 54, 142-143, 156
economic, family of, 38
enterprise asset-changes in, 88
formulation of, 9, 13: Chambers'
illustration of, 57; criteria for,
57; evaluation of, standards for,
need for, 56; Littleton's subsequent reliance on, 145; mathematical emphasis in, 156; summary of, 143-145

justification for, search for, 28
literature on, 56-72
Paton-Littleton monograph, 86, 97
practice and, 28, 157
scientific method as standard for,
142
value as element in, 38, 96, 128
Thinking, academic vs. practical,
157
Time reference, Postulate Y-4, 125
Transaction, 36, 91, 133
Transformability, criteria for, 33
Truth
coherence view of, 41, 52
correspondence theory of, 52
self-evident, 75
warranted, 51-52
whole and complete, 40-41

Utilization
measurements of, 38
of resources, 77, 81

Valuation, 77-78, 91, 99, 133, 145
Value
in accounting theory, 38, 96, 128
change in, measurement of, 132
common denominator of, 92: Postulate Z-4, 125
and continuity concept, 91
cost theory of, 96
economic, 122, 127
enterprise, 90, 133
events, influence of, 132-133
of future income, 78
net realizable, 122
relative emphasis on, 122, 145
scientific method and, 29
unamortized historical costs and,
77-78, 87, 122
Value-in-exchange, 93
Variable costing, 94
Vatter, William J., 122, 128, 158
Vienna Circle, 47, 51

Warrantability
of accounting propositions, 3-4,
21, 27, 29, 89
of assertions and truth, 51-52:
tests for, 75, 129
in Dewey's theory of inquiry, 30,
35, 37, 46-49, 57, 95, 109, 111,
123, 129, 142
statistical validity, 158
Weinberg, Julius Rudolph, 39, 51
White, Morton, 51
Whitehead, Arthur E., 46
Witschey, Robert E., 155